EFT Tapping Statements for Weight + Food Cravings, Anger, Grief, Not Good Enough, Failure

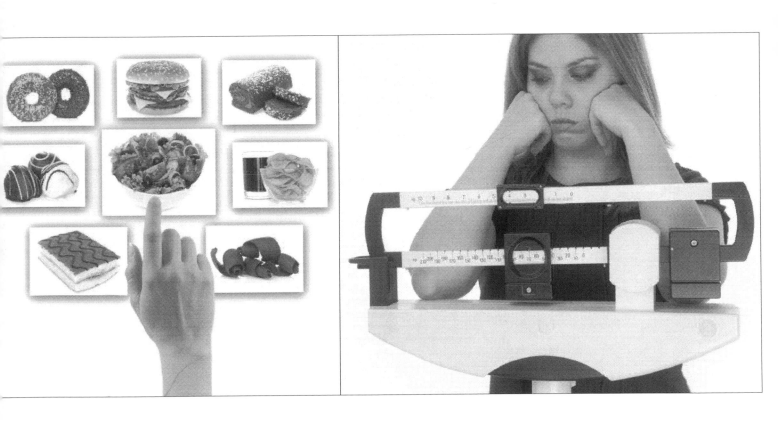

By

TESSA CASON

Tessa Cason
5694 Mission Ctr. Rd. #602-213
San Diego, CA. 92108
www.TessaCason.com
Tessa@TessaCason.com

TABLE OF CONTENTS

TABLE OF CONTENTS (CONTINUE)

Holding on to extra weight often serve as a person's unconscious anesthetic against stress, hurt, disappointment, failure, pain, as well as romantic attention, love, and success. It keeps many on the sidelines of life.

Bob Greene

Intro for
Weight + Cravings, Anger, Grief
Not Good Enough, Failure

The overweight and obesity rates have increased dramatically in the last 30 years and are expected to continue to increase year after year after year. More than two out of three Americans are overweight. Globally, 34% of the population is overweight. The weight loss industry is a $61+ billion dollar industry and still obesity is on the rise.

The usual weight loss programs aren't working. **Huge clue:** Appx. 95% of people that lose weight, put it right back on.

Though billions of dollars are spent each year to heal the obesity issue, it still persists. The reason? Weight is the SYMPTOM. NOT THE CAUSE. NOT THE ISSUE. The usual programs for weight loss aren't working because they are attempting to solve the problem by dealing with the symptoms instead of healing the cause.

There are a number of reasons that we overeat and are overweight. We eat
* for comfort
* to numb out
* out of boredom
* for pleasure
* to stuff feelings
* to suppress feelings
* for reward
* for love
* and the list goes on...

These reasons are symptoms.

Excess weight, food cravings, emotional eating, and overeating are symptoms of deeper unresolved issues beneath the weight. Attempting to solve the problem by only dealing with the symptoms is ineffective and does not heal the issue.

IF WE WANT TO HEAL OUR WEIGHT ISSUES, WE NEED TO HEAL THE CAUSE...
THE DYSFUNCTIONAL BELIEFS AND EMOTIONS.

IF WE WANT TO TRANSFORM OUR LIVES, WE NEED TO CHANGE THE
DYSFUNCTIONAL BELIEFS AND EMOTIONS ON THE SUBCONSCIOUS LEVEL.

ONE OF THE DEEPER ISSUES, BENEATH THE WEIGHT, IS SELF-LOVE.

During World War II, babies in orphanages died even though they received enough food. Their death was the result of not being loved, held, touched, comforted, and/or stroked. As infants, to survive, we are dependent upon others to love, comfort, stroke, and hold us.

For survival, when we don't love ourselves, we are dependent on others to show us love and to make us feel loved, lovable, and accepted. If we don't believe we are lovable, will we believe that anyone else would find us lovable? If someone did find us lovable, would we believe them? If they found us lovable, would we question their judgment or maybe their intent?

OVEREATING IS THE SYMPTOM.
EATING UNTIL WE ARE STUFFED IS THE SYMPTOM.
EATING TO SUPPRESS OUR EMOTIONS IS THE SYMPTOM.
EATING TO NUMB OUT IS THE SYMPTOM.

THE CAUSE IS LACK OF SELF-LOVE. THE RESULT IS EXCESS WEIGHT.

TO HEAL OUR WEIGHT ISSUES WE HAVE TO LEARN HOW TO BE INTIMATE WITH OURSELVES
AND RELEASE THE DYSFUNCTIONAL BELIEFS THAT PREVENT US FROM DOING SO.

If the various weight loss program haven't healed the obesity issue, acknowledging the problem has not healed the obesity issue, having an ah-ha awareness hasn't healed the obesity issue, talk therapy hasn't healed the issue, then how do we heal the obesity issue? How do we learn to love ourselves? How do we change the dysfunctional beliefs on a subconscious level?

Great question. Read on...

Today's Lesson: Self Love

THE POWER OF THREE

Issues that are difficult to heal are usually "locked in" and all three facets of the issue need to be cleared together to heal the issue.

EXCESS WEIGHT:

Cause – Lack of self love and the shame that we are not lovable or good enough to be loved.

Result – Overeating, eating to suppress emotions...to suppress anger, grief, and hurt that we are depended on others to shows us love, to make us feel lovable, and that we are good enough to be loved.

If we don't love ourselves, would we believe someone else that tells us they love us? Who could really love a defective, flawed, damaged human being such as us?

THE LOCKED IN EMOTIONS WITH WEIGHT ARE ANGER AND GRIEF.

When we don't love ourselves, we feel like such failures and that we are not good enough.

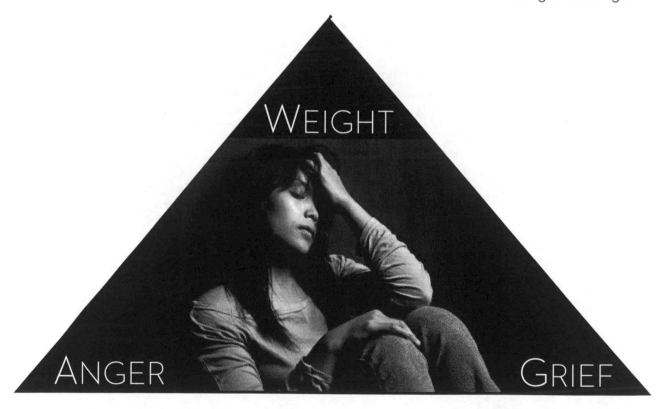

OUR BEHAVIOR IS GOVERNED BY...

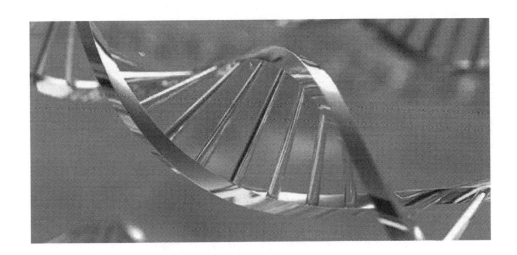

OUR BEHAVIOR IS GOVERNED BY...

Your significant-other tells you the two of you have to talk. "Oh no," you think! "He's going to end our relationship. It's over. How can that be? I love him sooooo much! I don't want it to be over! What am I going to do if it is over?" Oh, poor-woe-is-me as the back of your hand lands on your forehead.

Interesting reaction...assuming the worst, that the relationship will end. Let's examine this reaction:

One of your basic need is CONNECTION, TO BELONG, AND ROMANCE. Another basic need is SECURITY.

Both of your basic needs seem to be threatened, you respond with your number one pay-off, self-pity..."Oh poor woe is me."

OUR REACTIONS AND ACTIONS, THOUGHTS AND FEELING,
CHOICES AND DECISIONS ARE BASED ON OUR BELIEFS.

With the beliefs, "I'm not deserving of someone so wonderful," "Everything is going so well, I'm waiting for the other shoe to drop and for him to end the relationship," you assumed the worst. You assumed he were going to end the relationship.

When you sit down on the sofa together he says, "We have to talk about what we are doing for the holidays. Your family or mine?"

"Whoa," you think a little surprised and embarrassed. "The relationship isn't ending. He's talking about events to come that haven't happened yet!"

Our behavior is governed by our NEEDS and PAY-OFFS and the BELIEFS underneath the NEEDS and PAY-OFFS. All of our actions and reactions come down to the NEED(S) and PAY-OFF(S) and the BELIEFS underneath.

Our Basic Needs...

There are a number of different theories in regards to the Basic Human Needs. For simplicity, this section will cover Tony Robbins' 6 Basic Needs. Tony believes that to make any change in our lives, we need to understand how the situation meets our 6 basic needs.

The 6 Basic Human Needs are:

NEED #1	NEED #2	NEED #3
Certainty	Uncertainty	Accomplishment
Stability	Suspense	Importance
Safety	Surprise	Significance
Security	Variety	Feeling Unique
Consistency	Instability	Feel Needed
Order	Adventure	Achievement
Predictability	Challenges	Fulfillment

NEED #4	NEED #5	NEED #6
Connection	Growth	Service
Belong	Learning	Contribution
Unity	Constantly	Giving
Warmth	developing	Philanthropy
Romance	emotionally,	Making a
Togetherness	intellectually,	difference.
Friendships	and spiritually.	

The first four needs are essential for human survival. We all must have these needs met on some level to some extend. The last two are essential for fulfillment. Of these six needs, there are two that we experience so intensely that we will do almost anything to meet those needs. When we identify our two most important needs, we can discover our driving motivation and what gives meaning and motion to our lives.

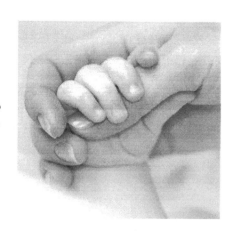

Thinking about television shows...they hook us in with the suspense (need #2). If it's a show that we follow, we feel connected to the characters (need #4). We know the main character (most likely) will not be killed off which provides us with certainty (need #1). Three of our six needs are being met when we watch television!

We can meet our 6 needs in positive or negative ways. For example, we can meet the need for significance by accomplishing something great or we can make ourselves feel significant by criticizing someone else's accomplishments – same need, different way of achieving it.

Even though we each have the same basic needs, they play out differently in our lives.

We might crave and need some uncertainty, excitement, and suspense in our lives. Yet, too much uncertainty could create fear. Not enough excitement and we become bored.

Some people want a lot of togetherness. For someone else, this much togetherness could be stifling and suffocating. Not enough connection and we might feel alone and separate from others.

On a scale of 1 – 10 with ten high, rate each need in it's importance in your life. Then on the right side, list them in the order with the highest at the top. (Might be helpful to have those significant-others in your life do this exercise as well.)

_____ Certainty, stability, security, consistency.	1. _____
_____ Uncertainty, suspense, variety, surprise.	2. _____
_____ Connection, unity, belonging, warmth.	3. _____
_____ Important, unique, significant, worthy of love.	4. _____
_____ Growth, learning.	5. _____
_____ Service, contribution, making a difference.	6. _____

Pay-offs for Not Creating Our Reality

Why would we **not** want to create a successful reality? Why would we **not** want success, happiness, peace, fulfillment, and love?

Instead of success and happiness, **we are seduced by pain and suffering**. In our society, we have a belief, "No pain, no gain." Usually we don't change until our backs are against the wall, until we've reached "rock bottom," when change becomes a must.

There are **"pay-offs"** for not creating a successful, prosperous, fulfilling, and joyful reality. Usually we have **one or two that is our go-to pay-off.**

Families have a pay-off that run in the families that might also play out in our lives as well. Might not be our first go-to pay-off but pops up every now and then.

Pay-off #1 – Avoidance

We would rather avoid...success, failure, being loved, loving, being alone, being with others, risks, challenges, responsibilities, obligations, fears, hurt, commitment, disappointment, contentment, being seen, being judged, and the list goes on.

Take success, for instant. Think back to all the statements you have heard about success. "It's lonely at the top." "How will you know who your friends are?" Your "friends," do they want to be with you because of you, the person you are or because of your success and what it would mean for them?

What about Personal Power? "Power corrupts." "Powerful people are conceited, ruthless, driven, thoughtless, and self-centered." Why would anyone want to be powerful?

"You can't have it all." "Money brings nothing but unhappiness." "Money is the root of all evils." "Will you remember me when you get rich and famous?" "What would I do with the money? I don't know anything about investing. I'm not smart enough to figure it out."

Are you a good steward of money? If you had financial wealth, would you spend it wisely? Would you be responsible and accountable? Is it okay to say "no" to someone in need and less fortunate than yourself? Does saying "no" make you selfish, incite insults that you are thinking of no one but yourself? Do you just avoid the whole scenario?

I had a client that had inherited $500,000 and became very popular. Six months later, he had less than before he received his inheritance. His bottom line? It was not okay for him to have more than anyone else. When his new friends asked for something, he would fulfill their wish and/or need. He bought one person a $30,000 car. Another asked for money for a down payment on a house. For another he paid their school tuition. When all the money was gone, so were the friends. When he was evicted from his apartment, the person he gave the down payment to for a house would not even let this man live with him.

Pay-off #1 is Avoidance. What am I avoiding? What failure am I avoiding? What success am I avoiding? Am I avoiding the responsibility of success? Am I avoiding obligations? Fears? Challenges? Anger?

When we do not feel we have the tools and skills to manage our lives, finances, successes, and/or relationships, we will avoid taking action, making decisions, moving forward in our lives, and/or getting involved in relationships. Avoidance.

PAY-OFF #2 - BLAME

You know the kind...they are always pointing the finger of blame at someone or something else other than themselves. It is never their fault. Never! The words "accountable" and "responsible" are not even in their vocabulary.

How many times have you heard, "I am the way I am because of my screwed up parents." "It's your fault! Not mine." "I thought you took care of it." "My boss treats me as if I am worthless." "My spouse does not want me to do that."

Pay-off #2 - Blame...We blame others for our failures. It is easier to blame others than to take responsibility, to take an honest look at ourselves. There is always someone else or God/Goddess that can be blamed. It is always someone else's fault.

Victim. Hopeless. Helplessness. Powerless. Lack of self-reliance, self esteem, and self-confidence. Seemingly, without any options. Someone else has the power and control. Someone else is in control of them and their life. Refusal to take responsibility. Not willing to be accountable. Unreliable. Stuck in the denial.

Pay-off #3 - Self-pity

"Oh, poor woe is me! No one loves me. No one to help me. I have to do this all by myself. I do everything for them and they do nothing for me! No one cares about me! Nothing ever goes my way. Life has always and will always be a struggle. I never get any breaks in life"...and on and on...

Another victim...everything is hopeless. Their situation is helpless. No one can help them. If someone offered to help, they would refuse with a number of reasons why someone could not help them. Only they can do it right. No one else would be able to figure it out. It is their "responsibility" so they have to do it themselves. If they let someone else help, it would not be done correctly. They would have to redo it so they might as well do it. They turn down any and all help and then feel sorry for themselves that they have to do the work themselves.

Pay-off #3 - Self-pity. Victim. Martyr. Helpless. Life is hopeless. If things were great, too much would be required of them.

Pay-off #4 - Guarantee

"Promise me, if I love you, you will never hurt me, abandon me, or reject me. You will marry me, love me forever and ever, and we will live happily ever after. When you do, then I will love you."

Wanting a guarantee is usually a biggie. "Promise me, if I try, I will succeed. I won't fail. I won't look stupid. I will succeed the first time. I will be a hero. Others will admire me."

Many people reach that fork in the path...one would take them to their heart's desire, fulfillment, and contentment. The second path, more traveled, takes them down a path of mediocrity that lacks passion, excitement, and joy but will pay the bills.

If one sets out on the first path, toward their heart's desires and their dreams, if they tried and did not succeed, there would be tremendous pain, disappointment, and embarrassment. Everyone knew they had charted their course and set sail. Everyone knew their intentions and hopes. If they failed, they would look foolish, incompetent, and stupid in the eyes of those that love and admire them.

Or maybe when they reach their goal they will discover the goal did not bring the joy and fulfillment they thought it would. All that work, planning, and sacrificing they would have to do and joy was not the prize. How sad and unhappy they would be. How disillusioned they would feel. So, why even try?

Pain, disappointment, embarrassment, disillusionment...is it really worth the risk? But, with a guarantee that they would accomplish their heart's desire and be a hero, most likely, they would take the first path toward their dreams and heart's desire.

Pay-off #4 – Guarantee...wanting a promise it will work. We hold out for the guarantee even though we know there are no guarantees. We don't create our reality because we don't have a guarantee.

PAY-OFF #5 – SELF-RIGHTEOUS/ANGER

Some people would rather be angry than to be at peace. Somehow, they think there is power in being angry. Being at peace is submissive and weak. If they were nice, they would be used and abused. Vulnerability is a handicap, not a strength!

These are the people that constantly complain. Nothing is ever right. They never direct their comments to someone that has the power to solve and/or resolve their problem. They would rather find fault with what they perceive as not being right. They have all the answers. But no one has ever asked them for the solution.

Anger is their defense. "Life is cruel and harsh. There are no free lunches." Anger is the mechanism they use to push others out of their lives. They don't want anyone to see the true them for fear of rejection. They use their anger as a manipulation to control others. They would rather be sarcastic and cynical than be vulnerable.

Pay-off #5: Self-Righteous/Anger...righteous so to feel hurt and/or angry. Refusal to resolve the hurt and anger. Wanting to feel hurt. Wanting to feel angry. Wanting to have the **right** to feel angry. This pay-off is about "angers" that they won't do anything about. If they really wanted to let go of the anger, they would do something about it.

PAY-OFF #6 - SELF-IMPORTANCE

These people find their importance in life by being the worst of the worst and/or grander than the best. When you are relating an incident that happened to you, they are the type that have to top your story with a story that is twice as horrendous or magnificent as yours. They have to outdo everything you do, compete with you...even though you were never competing or in competition with them in any way. They have to be better than you by either being the worst of the worst or the grandest of the grand.

In 2000, a woman asked if she paid my way, would I be her roommate on a two week trip to Peru with a spiritual teacher? Soon after departing, I was quick to realize why 5 of her friends declined the same offer. She had a morphine pump in her spine, feeding her morphine 24-hours a day. With everyone that sat down at her table for a meal, she went into her whole, painful medical history and problems.

Picture this: Machu Picchu, sunrise service with a shaman, she has a coughing fit. Does she remove herself from the group, walk away? No. Seven people went to her aid, offering water, cough drops, Reiki, to walk her over to an area where she could sit. She remained in the crowd, refusing any help...all while the shaman is still trying to conduct the ceremony.

Pay-off #6 - Self Importance...better than...worse than. Always a competition. Always proving how important they are. Always wanting the spotlight.

PAY-OFF #7 - CLINGING TO THE PAST

Moving forward in our lives can be frightening, scary, and not at all fun. The unknown of the future can create a great deal of stress within us, particularly if we do not think we have the tools and skills to handle what needs to be accomplished.

Childhood was so much easier when we were daddy's little princess or mom's favorite. We had a roof over our head, food in the refrigerator. We were cared for, financially supported, and loved unconditionally. Then the time came when we had to grow up, leave home, and go out into the big, frightening world...all on our own...as adults.

By clinging to the past we don't have to risk moving forward and failing. We don't have to be courageous, confident, or discerning. We don't have to face challenges or make decisions. We can blame our incompetence on fear instead of an unwillingness to learn new skills. We don't have to be truthful to ourselves about the depth of our character.

Imagine if Thomas Edison, Alexander Bell, Bill Gates, or Steven Jobs clung to the past. There would be no electricity, telephones, or software for our computers. By clinging to the past, we cheat ourselves of life, new adventures, developing new skills, discovering new facets of ourselves.

The very things we now wish that we could hold onto and keep safe from change were themselves originally produced by changes. And many of those changes, in their day, looked just as daunting as any in the present do. No matter how solid and comfortable and necessary the status quo feels today, it was once new, untried, and uncomfortable. Change is not only the path ahead, but it is also the path behind us.

William Bridges

BELIEFS AND THE SUBCONSCIOUS MIND

EVERYTHING IN OUR LIFE IS A DIRECT RESULT OF OUR BELIEFS.

A belief is a mental acceptance of and conviction in the truth, actuality, or validity of something. It is what we believe to be true, whether it is Truth or not. A belief is a thought that influences energy all the time.

A mis-belief, a dysfunctional belief is a belief that takes us away from peace, love, joy, stability, acceptance, and harmony. It causes us to feel stressed, fearful, anxious, and/or insecure.

The reason we aren't successful, happy, or prosperous has to do with our beliefs. Our beliefs determine our thoughts and feelings. Our thoughts and feelings determine our choices and decisions as well as our actions and reactions. Beliefs, then, precede all of our thoughts, feelings, choices, decisions, actions, reactions, and experiences.

Beliefs **precede** all of our thoughts, feelings, decisions, choices, actions, reactions, and experiences...

Our beliefs **determine** our thoughts.
Our thoughts **determine** our feelings.
Our thoughts and feelings **determine** our choices and decisions.
Our thoughts and feelings **determine** our actions and reactions.

Can you determine someone's beliefs from their actions and reactions? Persons A, B, C, and D just received a compliment that they looked nice today.

Person A responds:

Person B responds:

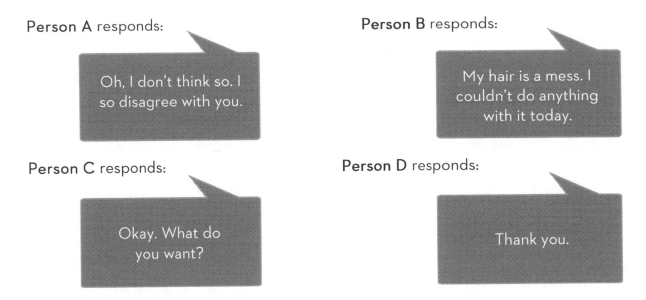

Oh, I don't think so. I so disagree with you.

My hair is a mess. I couldn't do anything with it today.

Person C responds:

Person D responds:

Okay. What do you want?

Thank you.

Person A: Totally disagrees. They don't think they look nice today. Person A definitely has self-esteem and self-worth issues. When we are not able to accept a compliment, it's a slap in the face for the person giving the compliment. It's as if Person A is saying, "If you think I look nice, your opinion sucks."

Person B: Cannot nor will not accept the compliment. They defect the compliment with a reason why they couldn't look nice. They justify their reason for not accepting the compliment. Think there might be a little bit of anger and/or shame in this type of response?

Person C: They think there are strings attached to the compliment. Anyone that would compliment them must want something. Might trust and discernment be an issue for them?

Person D: Well, if the response is genuine, then we know they have a healthy self-esteem and self-worth. If the response was said with arrogance, like "Naturally I look nice today" then we could either have someone who really is arrogant or someone who is insecure and using arrogance to hide the insecurity.

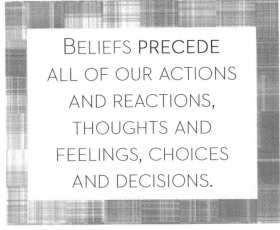

BELIEFS PRECEDE ALL OF OUR ACTIONS AND REACTIONS, THOUGHTS AND FEELINGS, CHOICES AND DECISIONS.

Subconscious Mind

The Conscious Mind

The conscious mind is that part of us that thinks, passes judgements, makes decisions, remembers, analyzes, has desires, and communicates with others. It is responsible for logic and reasoning, understanding and comprehension. The mind determines our actions, feelings, thoughts, judgements, and decisions **based on the beliefs.**

The Subconscious Mind

The subconscious is the part of the mind that is responsible for all of our involuntary actions like heart beat and breathing rate. It does not evaluate, make decisions, or pass judgment. It just is. It does not determine if something is "right" or "wrong."

The subconscious is much like the software of a computer. On the computer keyboard, if we press the key for the letter "a," we will see the letter "a" on the screen, even though we may have wanted to see "t."

Just as a computer can only do what it has been programmed to do, we can only do as we are programmed to do. Our programming is determined by our beliefs.

Our beliefs and memories are stored in the subconscious.

If we want to make changes in our lives, we have to change the programming, the mis-beliefs in the subconscious.

3 Rules of the Subconscious Mind

Three rules of the subconscious mind include:

1. Personal. It only understands "I," "me," "myself." First person.

2. Positive. The subconscious does not hear the word "no." When you say, "I am not going to eat that piece of cake," the subconscious mind hears "Yummm! Cake! I am going to eat a piece of that cake!"

3. Present time. Time does not exist for the subconscious. The only time it knows is "now," present time. "I'm going to start my diet tomorrow." "Tomorrow" never comes thus the diet is never started.

Three Rules of the
Subconscious Mind

Personal

Positive

Present Time

HEALING AND TRANSFORMATION

OUR COMFORT ZONE

It seems as we move forward in our lives, we reach a point when we want to change our lives we hit a brick wall, an invisible fence, a scratch in the vinyl record.

Have you heard of the electronic dog fences? An electronic fence uses a small electrical charge to keep a dog in a contained area. A transmitter emits a signal along an underground wire. When a dog nears the invisible boundary, their collar will sound a warning tone. If the dog continues, the dog will receive a mild static charge. It's harmless but just uncomfortable enough to teach the dog the new boundary.

Some of us remember vinyl records. We protected the records for fear of the record being scratched. Once the record was scratched, the needle would not move beyond the scratch. It would either play the same groove over and over and over or throw the needle backwards each time it tried to cross the scratch.

We have our invisible fences as well. It's called our comfort zone. We have scratches in our vinyl record. It's call a rut! If we want to change, we might get zapped by the electrical charge that we would feel if we climbed out of our comfort zone!

Freedom exists on the other side of the boundary and the scratch! We just don't know that freedom exists. We only know when we step outside our comfort zone we will be zapped.

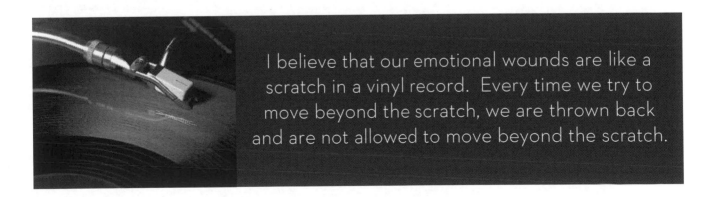

I believe that our emotional wounds are like a scratch in a vinyl record. Every time we try to move beyond the scratch, we are thrown back and are not allowed to move beyond the scratch.

Present Time

We can only heal when we are in Present Time.

When we are in present time, we feel alive, peaceful, and joyful. The world is bright. We **know** the truth. We **know** the answers to the questions we have been asking. We know the actions that must be taken. Our intuition is on target.

When we are not in present time, we are either in anger or fear, our regrets or worries. Anger, resentment, jealousy, and hurt keep us in the past. Fear, worry, doubt, and anxiety pull us into the future. Struggles, conflicts, "shoulds," "musts," judgments, and resistances pull us out of present time. All of these states of mind seem very real yet are illusions. The decisions and actions we make and take when we are not in present time are based on illusions.

Dragging or Energized?

When we are in present time only 5% - 10% of the time, we are dragging. Our energy is low. We can't stay awake. Being present 15%-20% of the time isn't much better. We are somewhat tired and sleepy. When we are in present time 90% of the time, we are awake, alert, rockin' & rollin'.

I'm draggin'.

Ways to Get Present

How can we be in present time when we choose? The obvious are sports, art, and playing a musical instrument. The not-so-obvious are acceptance, laughter, unconditional love, gratitude, forgiveness, and prayer.

Laughter, the Best Medicine

It is said that laughter is the best medicine. Laughter brings us into present time. We can only heal when we are in present time. To "get" a joke, we have to be in present time. A speaker will start their talks off with a joke. This brings their audience into the present, out of their thoughts, worries, concerns, and they are now able to concentrate on the speaker.

IS IT NECESSARY TO RELIVE THE PAIN IN ORDER TO HEAL OUR PAIN?

No.

Those suffering from PTSD (Post-traumatic Stress Disorder), do they need to relive the events that created the stress to heal? No.

You failed an important test. Do you have to relive the failure to heal? No.

Your boyfriend breaks up with you. Do you have to relive the break-up to heal? No.

What needs to be examined, explored, and healed are the thoughts and beliefs that contributed to the situation. Example: Your boyfriend ended the romantic relationship with you. Once again, you feel as if your heart has been stomped on. To heal, the beliefs you have about a romantic relationship need to be explored and healed.

* Are you deserving of a wonderful, loving relationship? Or do you settle?
* Are you extremely needy in relationships? Or distance and unattached?
* Do you share yourself and/or the "real" you with them? Or do you believe you would be rejected if they knew the real you?
* Do the people you want not want you?
* Do you end up in relationships with commitment-phobia people?
* Do you like the person that is wounded and needs to be healed?
* Do you date people that are unattainable, married, or just inappropriate?

The dysfunctional thoughts and beliefs that lead to the situation need to be examined, explored and healed.

WHY WE MIGHT HOLD ONTO EMOTIONAL PAIN

Emotional healing, healing our broken heart, is not a simple matter. When our heart is broken, we feel as if our heart has been shattered in a million pieces and it will never be whole again. We will never ever be whole again.

Time does not heal all. Emotional healing requires a conscious desire and effort on our part to put all the pieces back together again. It requires hope that tomorrow will be better than today... that the next minute will be better than this minute.

Why would we hold onto emotional pain? Sometimes we hold onto emotional pain because:

* We do not know how to let it go, how to move on, and/or how to heal the pain of the heart.

* We want to remain "connected" to that which caused our pain...the death of a loved one, the ending of something we did not want to end.

* We cannot and/or will not forgive. (We remain connected to those that we are not able to forgive.)

* We are afraid if we let the pain go, we are letting the loved one go as well. If we let go, we will forget and we do not want to forget.

* We feel if we heal our pain it is letting those that created our pain "off the hook."

* We benefit from a pay-off to remain in the pain; pay-off of blaming, avoiding, feeling sorry for ourselves, and/or staying angry.

* This is all we feel we deserve.

* We believe this is as good as it gets. Our lives won't get any better no matter how much work we do on ourselves.

* We don't think we can move through the pain.

* We can't find our way out of the pain by ourselves and we won't and/or don't ask for the help we need.

* It is our identity. Who would we be without our pain?

* It is easier to stay in the pain than to do anything about it.

MIND CHATTER – A VALUABLE TOOL!

Before I move on to how to heal and what to process, I want to discuss our Mind Chatter... which is a fabulous tool for knowing **what** to process.

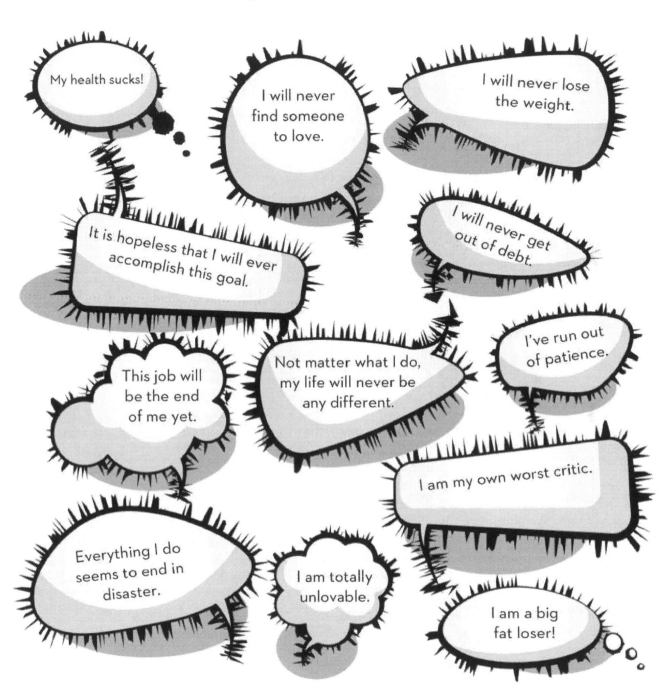

Mind chatter...that constant stream of thoughts that seem to have little value other than to possibly distract us. Most people think of mind chatter as something negative. I disagree. Mind chatter can be a very valuable tool for growth, healing, and learning about ourselves.

DOES YOUR MIND CHATTER GO SOMETHING LIKE THIS?

"I will never accomplish this goal."
"I will never find someone to love."
"I will never lose the weight."
"This job will be the end of me yet."
"My health sucks."
"I will never get out of debt."
"I am my own worst critic."
"I've run out of patience."
"Everything I do seems to end in disaster."

If the desire is personal growth, to learn, grow, and thrive, then maybe mind chatter is attempting to point out that which is **preventing us** from learning, growing, and thriving.

"I WILL NEVER ACCOMPLISH THIS GOAL."
  * Is the issue about hope?
  * The skills and abilities to accomplish the goal?
  * Time management?

"I WILL NEVER FIND SOMEONE TO LOVE."
  * Is this about being vulnerable and the fear of being rejected?
  * Is it easier to say you will never find anyone rather than process your fears and insecurities?

"I WILL NEVER LOSE THE WEIGHT."
  * Weight is only a symptom of dysfunctional beliefs.
  * Are you willing to look at the anger?
  * Do you really want to be vibrant, visible, and present?

"THIS JOB WILL BE THE END OF ME YET."
  * Are you willing to put the work into creating your dream job?
  * What can you do to increase your enjoyment of the job you currently have?
  * Do you need additional training to be able to perform your job more effectively?

"MY HEALTH SUCKS."
  * Are you willing to change your lifestyle so your health doesn't suck?
  * What is the issue of focusing time, energy, and money on you?
  * If you don't take care of your body, where will you live?

"I WILL NEVER GET OUT OF DEBT."
  * What have you done to learn about money management?
  * Are you willing to curb your spending?
  * Are you willing to do whatever it takes to get out of debt?

"I AM MY OWN WORSE CRITIC."
  * Is this a form of self-punishment?
  * Do you find fault with yourself before anyone else can?
  * Is this a fear of success, prosperity, of moving forward with your life and all the scary things
    that can happen when you are successful, prosperous, and visible?

"EVERYTHING I DO SEEMS TO END IN DISASTER."
  * Everything? Is this an exaggeration or for real?
  * Does your importance come because everything you do ends in disaster?
  * Is this your identity, the disaster monster?

"I'VE RUN OUT OF PATIENCE."
  * At whom? Yourself? Is this a way to make yourself wrong?
  * Is this a temper tantrum because you aren't getting what you want?
  * Do you have the tools, skills, and abilities to do what you are doing differently to have a
    different outcome?

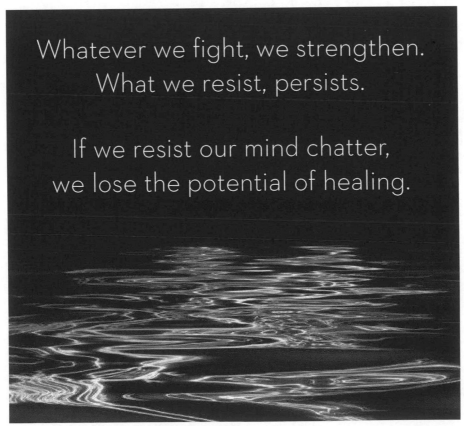

Whatever we fight, we strengthen.
What we resist, persists.

If we resist our mind chatter,
we lose the potential of healing.

How Do We Truly Transform Our Lives?

Other authors, teachers, and healers say:

* Change your thoughts to change your life.
* Change your daily routine to change your life.
* Change your habits to change your life.
* Say affirmation daily to change your life.
* Define and write out your goals to change your life.
* Change your attitude to change your life.
* Make different decisions to change your life.
* Write out an action plan and act on it now to make changes in your life.
* Change your personality to change your life.

Have not most of the information you read about changing your life included information like:

* You have to have a desire to change.
* You have to make a commitment to change.
* You have to be motivated.
* You have to know your purpose in life.
* You have to have a compelling future to move into.
* You have to have a plan.

You have tried changing your daily routine. That lasted for a short period of time. (82% of people that join a gym in January, have stopped going by February.) You have written down your goals, but they never happened. So you gave up on wanting or desiring anything.

You were committed to and motivated to change. You did have a compelling future to move into. You did have a plan. Yet, you are still the same today as you were when you were committed and motivated to change and had a plan.

Can we change by having an "ah-ha" moment? Can we change by having an awareness of our beliefs? Having an "ah-ha" does not necessarily mean change will be automatic. Having an awareness of what the issue is does not necessarily mean change will happen. Wanting and desiring change does not guarantee change will happen.

Example: You stumble over your shoelaces. Your **ah-ha** is "If my shoelaces were tied, I wouldn't have stumble over them!" You are **aware** your shoelaces are untied. You **want** your shoelaces to be tied. Yet, your shoelaces are still untied.

What about your reaction and response to your shoelace being untied? Do you get angry at yourself and tell yourself you should have tied them better? Do you make the shoelace wrong for coming untied?

When your life doesn't go as planned or expected, do you get angry, make yourself wrong? Blame someone or something else?

Does that resolve, solve, and heal the situation, the issue? Probably not.

BOTTOM LINE TO HEALING, CHANGING, AND TRANSFORMING OUR LIVES AND OUR BEHAVIOR IS THIS: THE DYSFUNCTIONAL BELIEFS MUST BE DELETED ON A SUBCONSCIOUS LEVEL. SIMPLE, RIGHT? (IF IT WAS SIMPLE, WE WOULD HAVE DONE IT A LONG TIME AGO!)

How do we know what our dysfunctional beliefs are? Excellent question. Our habits, behavior, thoughts, feelings, attitude, decisions, choices, and personality are excellent representation of what we believe (of what anyone believes). (It is true...actions speak louder than words).

All of our thoughts, feelings, attitudes, decisions, choices, routines, habits, and personality are all determined by our beliefs.

So, I've mentioned that everything comes down to needs and pay-offs. When a client asks why they or someone else did something, I ask them, "What was the need? What was the pay-off?" Our needs and pay-offs explain, 100% of the time, why we reaction or respond as we do as well as the actions we take.

Exploration, being the observer of our lives and of ourselves, (without judging or being critical of ourselves) is an important first step. Exploration and then awareness. Can we change if we explore our lives and have an awareness of what needs to change? Not quite.

Acknowledgement, taking ownership (which isn't always pleasant) is critical as well. We can't change something we don't take responsibility for as our own. (Blaming someone or something else for the circumstances of our lives will not change our lives. Blame is one of the pay-offs for not creating our reality.)

So, I've also mentioned a time or two that to truly change our lives, permanently-change-our-lives, our behavior, our thoughts, our feeling, decisions, choices, etc...we have to change the beliefs on the subconscious level. We have to change our programming in the subconscious. Our beliefs are "stored" in the subconscious.

HOW TO DO THAT? That was the object of my search at the beginning of my life coaching practice when my clients were not fulfilling their homework. I found a powerful tool called EFT Tapping that can change our dysfunctional emotions and beliefs on a subconscious level.

How do I know that it is powerful? I've witness the miraculous shifts and changes in my clients as well as myself.

In 2005, I was diagnosed with thyroid cancer. Two different labs came back with the result of cancer. Bummer. After deciding that I wanted to stick around for many more years and be healthy (if you don't take care of your body, where are you going to live?), I started tapping. The only change I made in my life between the diagnosis and surgery was to tap on the emotional significance of the thyroid.

In the recovery room, the surprised surgeon told me it was not cancer. Do I think I would be typing now if I had not tap? No. I do not think I would be. I know that tapping saved my life.

Healing is a Journey

Just recently I had a client, Serena, that had been diagnosed 2 years earlier with cancer. The doctors had given her 6 months to live. In her search for healing, she was doing a number of different processes and techniques, visiting a number of different healers, light workers, and counselors.

In one of Serena's sessions, she wanted to know if any of the various things she was doing was contributing to her longevity. With the criteria of longevity, we muscle tested the 60+ techniques, processes, light workers, and healers. The only process that was contributing to her longevity was EFT Tapping – Emotional Freedom Technique.

She said, "That doesn't surprise me. After doing everything and now doing EFT Tapping, I can feel the difference. In my sessions with you, I am looking at the dysfunctional beliefs that contributed to the cancer. Cancer is only the symptom. The mis-beliefs is the cause."

In hindsight, Serena realized the reason she had tried so many different techniques is that none of the techniques really looked at depth at her core issues. Intuitively, she knew that none of what she had done was the "one solution." It wasn't until she discovered EFT and changing the dysfunctional beliefs did she know what she was searching for.

Her last session she thanked me for the work we did together. She had wished she had found EFT two years earlier. She knew that looking at depth at her issues, pursuing one path, one technique, she would have been able to survive the cancer. Sadly, she died shortly after our last session.

Serena's shotgun effect in search of health was not effective. Healing requires an in-depth look at our dysfunctional beliefs and an in-depth look at our lives. Having a "system" and/or a coach or a therapist that takes us step-by-step toward our specific, desired outcome is most effective. Sometime it does require someone, preferable a therapist, outside our issues to help us recognize what we are not able to see on our own.

When we wander, seldom
do we make it to the target.

EFT Tapping
Emotional Freedom Technique
(A Powerful Tool To Change Our Lives)

EFT Tapping – Emotional Freedom Technique

If we want to make changes in our lives, long-lasting, permanent, constructive changes, we have to change the destructive, dysfunctional, mis-beliefs in the subconscious. We have to change the programming in the subconscious.

EFT Tapping changes dysfunctional, mis-beliefs on a subconscious level.

What is EFT – Emotional Freedom Technique:

EFT is a technique that allows us to change dysfunctional beliefs and emotions on a subconscious level. It involves making a statement while tapping different points along meridian paths.

The general principle behind EFT is that the cause of all negative emotions is a disruption in the body's energy system. By tapping on locations where a number of the different meridians flow, we are able to release unproductive memories, emotions, and beliefs which cause the blockages.

EFT Tapping Statements:

An EFT statement has three parts to it:

Part 1: Starts with "**Even though,**" followed by

Part 2: A statement which could be the **dysfunctional emotion or belief,** and

Part 3: Ends with "**I totally and completely accept myself.**"

A total statement would be "**Even though, I crave sweets, I totally and completely accept myself.**"

The instructions below are described if you were using your right hand. Reverse directions to tap using the left hand. It is only necessary to tap one side. Tapping both sides does not add any additional benefit.

I. BEGIN WITH CIRCLING OR THE KARATE CHOP POINT (SEE NEXT PAGE):

A. With the fingertips of your right hand, find a tender spot below your left collar bone. Once you have found the tender spot, with your right fingertips, press firmly on the spot, make a circular motion toward the left shoulder, toward the outside, clockwise.

B. As your fingers are circling and pressing against the tender spot, make the following statement 3 times: "Even though,____[mis-belief statement]____, I totally and completely accept myself." An example would be: "Even though, I fear change, I totally and completely accept myself."

II. TAPPING:

A. After the third time, tap the following 8 points repeating the [mis-belief statement] each time with each point. Tap each point 7 – 10 times:

1. The inner edge of the eyebrow just above the eye. [I fear change.]

2. Temple, just to the side of the eye. [I fear change.]

3. Just below the eye (on the cheekbone). [I fear change.]

4. Under the nose. [I fear change.]

5. Under the lips. [I fear change.]

6. Under the knob of the inside edge of the collar bone. [I fear change.]

7. 3" under the arm pit. [I fear change.]

8. Top back of the head. [I fear change.]

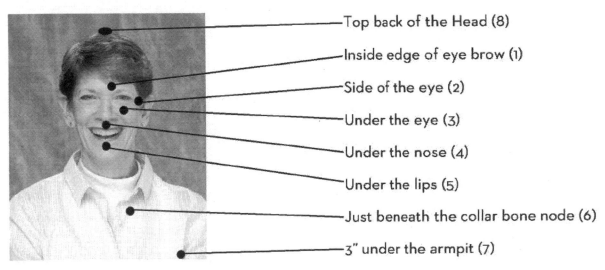

Top back of the Head (8)

Inside edge of eye brow (1)

Side of the eye (2)

Under the eye (3)

Under the nose (4)

Under the lips (5)

Just beneath the collar bone node (6)

3" under the armpit (7)

B. After tapping, take a deep breath. If you are not able to take a deep, full, satisfying breath, do eye rolls.

III. EYE ROLLS

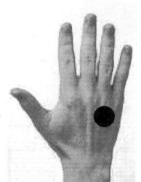

A. With one hand, tap continuously on the **back** of the other hand between the 4th and 5th fingers.
B. Head is held straight forward, eyes looking straight down.
C. For 6 seconds, roll your eyes from the floor straight up toward the ceiling while repeating the statement. Keep the head straight forward, only moving the eyes.

IV. TAKE ANOTHER DEEP BREATH.

KARATE CHOP POINT (KCP):

For the set up in EFT Tapping, use either the circling or the KCP. It is a matter of preference. One is not more effective than the other.

To tap the KCP, use the fingertips of the opposite hand or the KCP of both palms can be tapped together.

Tapping Points for the Short Form of EFT
Emotional Freedom Technique

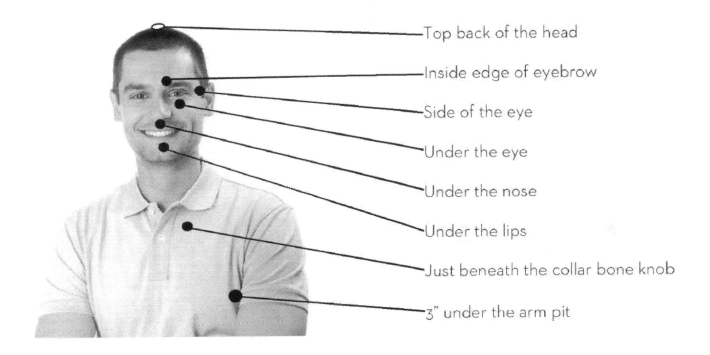

Top back of the head

Inside edge of eyebrow

Side of the eye

Under the eye

Under the nose

Under the lips

Just beneath the collar bone knob

3" under the arm pit

Yawning and Taking a Deep Breath

From Oriental medicine, we know that when Chi (energy) flows freely through the meridians, the body is healthy and balanced. Physical, mental, and/or emotional illness can result when the energy is blocked.

Dysfunctional beliefs and emotions produce blocks along the meridians, blocking energy from flowing freely in the body.

With EFT tapping, as we tap, we are releasing the blocks. As blocked energy is able to flow more freely, the body is now able to "breathe a sigh of relief." Yawning is that sigh of relief.

If, after tapping, we are able to take a complete, deep, full, and satisfying breath, we know that an EFT tapping statement has cleared. This yawn is an indication that an EFT tapping statement has cleared.

If the yawn or breath is not a full, deep breath then the statement didn't clear completely.

INTEGRATION...WHAT HAPPENS AFTER TAPPING

After tapping, our system needs some downtime for integration to take place. When the physical body and the mind are "idle," integration can then take place.

Sometimes, in the first 24 hours after tapping, we might find ourselves vegging more than normal, sleeping more than normal, or more tired than normal. This downtime is needed to integrate the new changes.

After installing a new program into our computer, sometimes we have to reboot the computer (shut down and restart) for the new program to be integrated into the system.

After tapping, our bodies need to reboot. We need some downtime. When we sleep, the new changes are integrated.

Healing begins naturally after the body has had a chance to integrate.

Sometimes after tapping, we forget the intensity of our pain and think that our feeling better had nothing to do with the tapping. Something so simple could not possibly create the improvement in our state of mind!

When we cut our finger, once it is healed, we don't even remember cutting our finger. As we move toward health, wealth, and well-being, sometimes we don't remember how unhappy, restless, or isolated we once felt.

How Does EFT Tapping Work?

1. ACCEPTANCE: The last part of the tapping statement we say, "I totally and completely accept myself." **Acceptance brings us into present time.** We can only heal if we are in present time. Laughter brings us into present time. "Laughter is the best medicine."

2. ADDRESSES THE CURRENT MIS-BELIEF ON A SUBCONSCIOUS LEVEL: In order to make changes in our lives, we have to change the dysfunctional beliefs, the mis-belief on a subconscious level. The middle part of the tapping statements are the "instructions" for the subconscious. **In order to make changes in our lives, we only care what the subconscious hears.**

3. PATTERN INTERRUPT: Dysfunctional memories and/or mis-beliefs disrupt or block the flow of energy from flowing freely along the meridians. Tapping is a pattern interrupt that disrupts the flow of energy to allow our **body's own Infinite Wisdom to come forth for healing.**

4. MIS-DIRECT: One role of the physical body is to protect us. When our hand is too close to a flame, the body automatically pulls the hand back to safety. An EFT Tapping statement that agrees with the current belief is more effective. The physical body is less likely to "sabotage" the tapping if it agrees with the current belief.

AN EXAMPLE: The very first tapping statement we need to tap is: "It is not okay or safe for my life to change." Even though our lives are constantly changing does not mean we are comfortable or okay with change. When we are not comfortable with change, it creates stress for the body.

EFT Tapping Statement: "It is not okay or safe for my life to change."

* This statement appeases the physical body since it agrees with the current belief.
* The subconscious hears, "It is okay and safe for my life to change."
* The tapping disrupts the energy flow so our Truth can come forth.

The body will always gravitate to health, wealth, and well-being when the conditions allow it. EFT Tapping weeds the garden so that the blossoms can bloom more easily and effortlessly.

SCIENCE AND EFT TAPPING RESEARCH

EFT has been researched in more than 10 countries by more than 60 investigators whose results have been published in more than 20 different peer-reviewed journals. Two of the leading researchers are Dawson Church, Ph.D. and David Feinstein, Ph.D.

Dr. Dawson Church, a leading expert on energy psychology and an EFT master, has gathered all the research information and can be found on this website: www.EFTUniverse.com.

TWO RESEARCH STUDIES DISCUSSED BELOW

HARVARD MEDICAL SCHOOL STUDIES AND THE BRAIN'S STRESS RESPONSE

Studies at the Harvard Medical School revealed that stimulating the body's meridian points significantly reduced activity in a part of the brain called the amygdala.

The amygdala can be thought of as the body's alarm system. When the body is experiencing trauma or fear, the amygdala is triggered and the body is flooded with cortisol also know as the "stress hormone." The stress response sets up an intricate chain reactions.

The studies showed that stimulating or tapping points along the meridians such as EFT tapping, drastically reduced and/or eliminated the stress response and the resulting chain reaction.

DR. DAWSON CHURCH AND CORTISOL REDUCTION

Another significant study was conducted by Dr. Daws on Church. He studied the impact an hour tapping session would have on the cortisol levels of 83 subjects. He also measured the cortisol levels of people who received traditional talk therapy and the cortisol levels of a third group who received no treatment at all.

On an average, for the 83 subjects that completed an hour tapping session, cortisol levels were reduced by 24% reduction. Some subjects experienced a 50% reduction in cortisol levels.

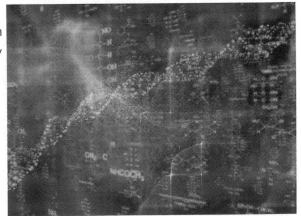

Subjects that completed an hour long traditional talk therapy and the subjects that had completed neither sessions did not experience any significant cortisol reduction.

Benefits of Using EFT Tapping

* The last part of the statement is "I totally and completely **accept** myself." **Acceptance** brings us into present time. Healing can only take place when we are in present time.

* By tapping, we are **calling forth our truths**. The key word here is "**our.**" Not anyone else's. If my name is "Lucas," tapping the statement "Even though my name is Troy," my name will not be changed to Troy.

* Tapping **calls forth our own body's Infinite Wisdom.** When we cut our finger, our body knows how to heal the cut itself. Once the dysfunctional emotions, experiences, and beliefs have been "deleted," our body **automatically** gravitates to health, wealth, wisdom, peace, love, joy...

* By changing the mis-beliefs and dysfunctional emotions on a subconscious level, the changes we make with EFT are **permanent.**

* By tapping, we are "**neutralizing**" the stored memories that have been blocking energy from flowing freely along the meridians.

* Another benefit of tapping and EFT is desensitization. Let's say, we have a difficult person in our life that ignores us and/or criticizes us and we tap the statement: "This difficult person [or their name] ignores and criticizes me."

Tapping doesn't mean they will no longer ignore and/or criticize us.

It can, though, **desensitize us** so we no longer are affected by their behavior. Once we are desensitized, our perception and mental thinking improves. We are better able to make informed decisions. We don't take and make everything personally. Our health is not negatively impacted. Our heart doesn't beat 100 beats/minute. Smoke stops coming out of our ears. And our faces don't turn red with anger and frustration.

WHEN TO USE EFT TAPPING AND
WHAT CAN EFT TAPPING CHANGE

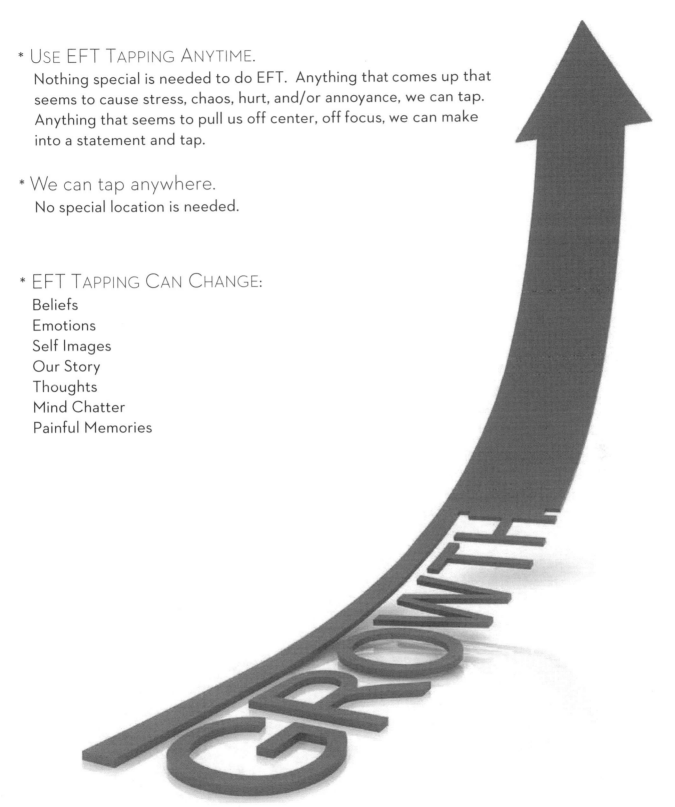

* USE EFT TAPPING ANYTIME.
  Nothing special is needed to do EFT. Anything that comes up that
  seems to cause stress, chaos, hurt, and/or annoyance, we can tap.
  Anything that seems to pull us off center, off focus, we can make
  into a statement and tap.

* We can tap anywhere.
  No special location is needed.

* EFT TAPPING CAN CHANGE:
  Beliefs
  Emotions
  Self Images
  Our Story
  Thoughts
  Mind Chatter
  Painful Memories

INTENSITY LEVEL

One measure of knowing how much an "issue" has been "resolved" is to begin, before tapping, by giving the issue an intensity number between 1 – 10, with 10 being high.

For example, you want a romantic partnership yet, you haven't met "the one." Thinking about the likelihood of a romantic relationship happening for you, how likely, on a scale of 1 – 10, with 10 being very likely and 1, not likely at all, would a romantic relationship happen for you?

Okay. You gave yourself a 2. Now let's start tapping!

When asked what the "issues" might be, "Well," you say. "It doesn't seem as if the people I want, want me."

Great tapping statement. So, you tap out, "Even though, the people I want don't want me, I totally and completely accept myself." After tapping you check in with yourself, the Intensity Level (IL) has gone up to a 4, a little bit more likely.

What comes to mind now? You say, "No one will find me desirable." Great tapping statement. You tap out, "Even though, no one will find me desirable, I totally and completely accept myself." Check the IL. How likely? Now you are at a 5. Cool! Progress.

What comes to mind now? You say, "I'm not comfortable being vulnerable in romantic relationships." Great tapping statement. You tap out, "Even though, I'm not comfortable being vulnerable in a romantic relationship, I totally and completely accept myself." Check the IL. Now it is a 6. Still progress.

What comes to mind now? "Well, it feels like if I am in a relationship, I will lose a lot of my freedom." Make this into a tapping statements. "Even though, I will lose my freedom when I am in a relationship, I totally and completely accept myself." The IL has gone up to a 7.

What comes to mind now? "Oh, if I was in a relationship, I would have to be accountable to someone!" Make this into a tapping statement: "Even though, I would have to be accountable to someone if I was in a relationship, I totally and completely accept myself." Wow…the IL is 9, very likely!

GIVING AN ISSUE AN INTENSITY LEVEL GIVES US AN INDICATION OF THE PROGRESS WE ARE MAKING WITH RESOLVING AND/OR HEALING THAT ISSUE IN OUR LIVES.

THE VERY FIRST EFT TAPPING STATEMENT TO TAP

The very first EFT tapping statement I have clients and students tap is "It is not okay or safe for my life to change." I have muscle tested this statement with more than a thousand people. Not one person tested strong that is was okay or safe for their life to change.

HOW EFFECTIVE CAN EFT OR ANY THERAPY BE IF IT ISN'T OKAY OR SAFE FOR OUR LIVES TO CHANGE?

Since our lives are constantly changing, if it is not okay or safe for our lives to change, every time our lives change, it creates stress for the body. Stress creates another whole set of issues for ourselves, our lives, and our bodies.

IT'S NOT OKAY OR SAFE FOR MY LIFE TO CHANGE.

USING A NEGATIVE EFT TAPPING STATEMENT

Our beliefs **precede** all of our thoughts, feelings, decisions, choices, actions, reactions, and experiences...

If we want to make changes in our lives, we have to change the mis-beliefs, the dysfunctional beliefs. Our beliefs are stored in the subconscious.

To change our lives, to change a belief, we only care what the subconscious hears when we tap. The subconscious does not hear the word "no." When we say, "I am not going to eat that piece of cake," the subconscious hears, "Yummm, cake!"

Example, if we don't believe we had what it takes to be successful and we tap the statement, "I have what it takes to be successful," the body could sabotage the tapping. We could tap and it won't clear.

If instead the statement we make is "I don't have what it takes to be successful," the **not** appeases the physical body and the subconscious hears, "I have what it takes to be successful!"

A STATEMENT WITH THE WORD "NO" OR "NOT," ALTHOUGH MAY SEEM TO BE CONTRADICTORY, WORKS BEST!

TAPPING FOR:
WHY WE MIGHT HOLD ONTO EMOTIONAL PAIN

On page 23, I listed 12 possible reasons we might hold onto emotional pain. Below are EFT tapping statements for emotional healing:

* I will never ever be whole again.

* My heart has been shattered into a million pieces.

* I will never be able to recover from this hurt.

* I don't know how to let my pain go.

* I don't know how to move on with my life.

* I don't know how to heal my broken heart.

* I'm not ready to let _____ [name or person or event that you do not want to let go] go.

* I'm not willing to forgive _____ [name of person and/or God].

* I'm afraid to let my pain go.

* I'm afraid I will forget _____ [name of person] if I let my pain go.

* I don't know who I would be without my pain.

* It's easier to stay in the pain than to do anything about it.

* I won't heal because it would let _____ [name of person] off the hook for creating my pain.

* I don't deserve to be loved, respected, or cherished.

* I don't deserve a life of health, wealth, and happiness.

* I don't ask for help with healing my heart.

* I can't make it through my emotional pain.

INNER CRITIC, NEGATIVE SELF-TALK?

Is using a negative in an EFT tapping statement parroting our negative self-talk, stimulating our inner critic?

Our inner critic and negative self-talk are our teachers. They are letting us know the path to healing, to well-being, and to peace. Since we ignore their words of wisdom, it seems as if the inner voice is critical and negative. It seems as if they are "nagging" us. The truth is this: They are pointing out what needs to be healed in order for us to be healthy, wealthy, happy, and wise!

We can make tapping statements out of the inner critic's pearls of wisdom (negative self-talk). For example, let's say the inner dialogue goes something like this, "I eat everything in sight. I can't stop eating."

If we tapped, "I can't stop eating," the subconscious hears "I can stop eating. I can stop eating. I can stop eating."

SUBCONSCIOUS DOES NOT HEAR THE WORD "NO."

The EFT tapping statement is more effective when it agrees with the current dysfunctional belief. The current belief is "I can't stop eating." The physical body is less likely to sabotage the process because the statement agrees with the current belief.

To make changes in our lives, lasting changes, we have to change the current dysfunctional belief in the subconscious. The subconscious does not hear the word "no." When we tap, "I can't stop eating," the subconscious hears "I can stop eating."

> The inner critic and negative self-talk are actually words of pearls shining light on the path that needs to be healed. "Nothing ever goes away until it teaches us what we need to know."
>
> Pema Chondron

Finishing Touches (Optional)

Part 1 of Finishing Touches - Read the statements on the following page. If one or more of the statements doesn't feel true yet, then you might want to do one round of the statements by inserting a "no" into the statement.

Part 2 - Some like to finish their tapping with statements that are centering and calming. If this is you, then you might want to try the following 16 statements and/or make up those that you like. The statements on the following page can be said in any order that works for you.

Tapping Location	Statement
Eyebrow	All is well in my life.
Temple	Every day in every way I am getting better and better.
Under the Eye	I am fulfilled in every way, every day.
Under the Nose	My blessings appears in rich appropriate form with divine timing.
Under the Lips	I am an excellent steward of wealth and am blessed with great abundance.
Under the Collarbone Knob	I take complete responsibility for everything in my life.
Under the Arm	I have all the tools, skills, and abilities to excel in my life.
Top back part of the Head	I know I will be able to handle anything that arises in my life.
Eyebrow	All my dreams, hopes, wishes, and goals are being fulfilled each and every day.
Temple	Divine love expressing through me, now draws to me new ideas.
Under the Eye	I am comfortable with my life changing.
Under the Nose	I am able to create all that I desire.
Under the Lips	I know what needs to be done and follow through to completion.
Under the Collarbone Knob	My health is perfect in every way, physically, mentally, emotionally, and spiritually.
Under the Arm	I invite into my subconscious Archangel Raphael to heal all that needs to be forgiven, released, and redeemed. Cleanse me and free me from it now.
Top back part of the Head	The light of God surrounds me. The love of God enfolds me. The power of God protects me. The presence of God watches over and flows through me.

This eBook covers the Basics of EFT Tapping. For a more complete guide to EFT Tapping, please download "Healing, Transformation, & All Things EFT Tapping" on my website:

www.TessaCason.com

HOW TO USE THIS BOOK

1. The statements are divided into sections. Read through the statements in one section. As you read a statement, notice if you have any reaction to the statement or feel the statement might be true for you. If so, circle the number for that statement.

2. Once you have completed reading all the statements in one section, go back and reread the statements you circled and rate them on a scale of 1 – 10, with 10 being a biggie."

3. On the following page, list the top statements.

4. From this list, select one and describe how it plays out in your life. It is important to recognize and identify the pattern. What are the consequences of having this mis-belief? Is there a trigger? How does it begin? How does it benefit you? How has it harmed you? There will be a different example listed in each section.

5. Tap out the statements. Statements can be combined for scripts...a different statement on each of the different tapping points in one round of tapping.

6. Describe any flashbacks or memories that you might have had as you were tapping out the statements. Describe any ah-has, insights, and/or thoughts you might have had as a result of tapping the statements.

7. After tapping all the statements, review them to determine if you still have a reaction to any of the statements. If you do, you have several options. One, put a "Why" before the statement. Tap out the answer. Secondly, note that this statement may not have cleared and continue on to the next section. Most likely, after additional statements are tapped, statements that may not have cleared, will clear without having to tap the statement again.

8. Allow some downtime for integration and for the body to heal.

9. The number of sections you do at a time will be up to you. Initially, you might want to do one section to determine if you get tired and need to some downtime for integration.

10. The day after tapping, again review the statements you tapped to determine if you still have a reaction. If you do, follow the instructions in #7.

Mis-belief Tapping Statements and Worksheet Pages for:

Weight + Food Cravings
Anger
Grief
Not Good Enough
Failure

WEIGHT & EMOTIONAL EATING

The identity of a person with excess weight is "I'm a fat person." This individual may diet and lose weight in the short term, but they will always gain it back. Their sense of certainty about who they are will guide their behaviors until the self is once again consistent with their identity. If the identity is that of a fat person, they will regain the weight to fulfill that identity. The self will fulfill our beliefs about ourselves even when they are destructive and disempowering.

Tony Robbins

Mis-belief Tapping Statements for Weight & Emotional Eating

1. Food is love.
2. Life is pointless.
3. It is scary to feel.
4. I don't live my life.
5. I feel empty inside.
6. Food is the enemy.
7. My life is pointless.
8. I don't honor my body.
9. Food is my only friend.
10. I lack clarity for my life.
11. Loving myself is selfish.
12. I don't accept my body.
13. I feel lost and hopeless.
14. I eat when I feel anxious.
15. I am obsessed with food.
16. I make poor food choices.
17. I stuff myself until it hurts.
18. I eat when I feel deprived.
19. Food makes me feel good.
20. I overeat when I am afraid.
21. I overeat when I am bored.
22. My eating is out of control.
23. I am tired of being fat but...
24. My focus is always on food.
25. I overeat when I feel lonely.

> The commonest form of malnutrition in the western world is obesity.
>
> Mervyn Deitel

1. From the previous page, list the seven statements that you thought or felt applied to you:

1.

2.

3.

4.

5.

6.

7.

2. Select one of the statements from above and describe how it plays out in your life. Give an example or two. It is important to recognize and identify the pattern. Is there a trigger? How does it begin? How has it benefited you? How has it harmed you? For instance, do you use food to feel loved? Does food = love? Is it easier to relate to food? Do you know how to relate to people? Is there a fear of possibly being rejected if you tried to connect with someone? Little chance of being rejected by food.

3. Tap the seven statements above. If more than seven applied, tap them as well.

4. As you were tapping, did you have any new thoughts, memories of the past surface, any additional insights, and/or an ah-ah awareness?

26. The only activity I enjoy is eating.
27. My thoughts center around food.
28. I overeat when I am stressed out.
29. I'm not willing to feel my feelings.
30. I am only happy when I am eating.
31. I overeat when I need comforting.
32. My thoughts center about dieting.
33. Food is a way of rewarding myself.
34. I can't be happy until I lose weight.
35. I eat without even tasting my food.
36. I will never be happy with my body.
37. Food is my only source of pleasure.
38. I eat for other reasons than hunger.
39. I know I eat out of frustrations but...
40. I am tired of being overweight but...
41. Food is a reward for good behavior.
42. I know I overeat to be invisible but...
43. My cravings are in control of my life.
44. I continue to eat even after I am full.
45. I am afraid to weigh my ideal weight.
46. Food is the one thing I can count on.
47. I know I eat to bury my feelings but...
48. I am not willing to delay gratification.
49. I overeat when happiness eludes me.
50. I am unaware of when and what I eat.

> Being overweight helps many fearful people feel as if they are invisible. They seek ways to sabotage themselves in order to return to the safety that their excess weight provides.
>
> Bob Greene

1. From the previous page, list the seven statements that you thought or felt applied to you:

1.

2.

3.

4.

5.

6.

7.

2. Select one of the statements from above and describe how it plays out in your life. Give an example or two. It is important to recognize and identify the pattern. Is there a trigger? How does it begin? How has it benefited you? How has it harmed you? For instance, are you tired of being overweight but...? Does that mean you will do anything about your weight? "But" erases everything in front of it. The truth comes after the "but."

3. Tap the seven statements above. If more than seven applied, tap them as well.

4. As you were tapping, did you have any new thoughts, memories of the past surface, any additional insights, and/or an ah-ah awareness?

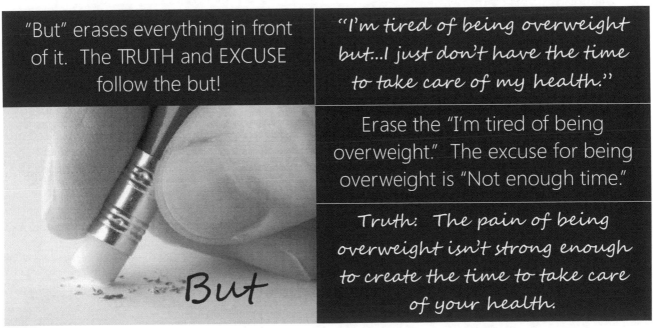

"But" erases everything in front of it. The TRUTH and EXCUSE follow the but!

"I'm tired of being overweight but...I just don't have the time to take care of my health."

Erase the "I'm tired of being overweight." The excuse for being overweight is "Not enough time."

Truth: The pain of being overweight isn't strong enough to create the time to take care of your health.

51. My health is not my priority.
52. I overeat when I am anxious.
53. I cannot imagine myself thin.
54. I have lost interest in my life.
55. Eating healthy food is boring.
56. I overeat when I am unhappy.
57. I overeat when I feel unloved.
58. I am not conscious when I eat.
59. I feel ashamed after I overeat.
60. I overeat when I feel rejected.
61. I'm no fun when I am on a diet.
62. I overeat when I am frustrated.
63. I don't know what I am craving.
64. I eat when I feel overwhelmed.
65. Once I start eating I can't stop.
66. I think about food all day long.
67. I only overeat when I am alone.
68. I overeat when I am depressed.
69. Eating healthy food is not filling.
70. I overeat when I feel humiliated.
71. It takes a huge effort to eat less.
72. I know I should lose weight but...
73. It is impossible for me to be thin.
74. I eat whether I am hungry or not.
75. I have no control over my eating.

> Dedication, commitment, and effort are needed to accomplish anything worthwhile. We need to work hard if we want to achieve success, to accomplish anything worthwhile. Losing weight and taking care of ourselves is no exception.
>
> Bob Greene

1. From the previous page, list the seven statements that you thought or felt applied to you:

1.

2.

3.

4.

5.

6.

7.

2. Select one of the statements from above and describe how it plays out in your life. Give an example or two. It is important to recognize and identify the pattern. Is there a trigger? How does it begin? How has it benefited you? How has it harmed you? For instance, is your health a priority? If health is not your priority, is it not okay or safe to put yourself first? Or is "taking care of everyone else" the excuse you use not to be responsible for your own health?

3. Tap the seven statements above. If more than seven applied, tap them as well.

4. As you were tapping, did you have any new thoughts, memories of the past surface, any additional insights, and/or an ah-ah awareness?

76. It is impossible for me to lose weight.
77. I overeat even when I am not hungry.
78. Food is available when I feel isolated.
79. Food is the solution when I am upset.
80. Food is a way of showing myself love.
81. I know I eat because I am bored but…
82. I am afraid to be visible and beautiful.
83. Food is the only way I nurture myself.
84. I use food to stuff down my emotions.
85. I don't know what is missing in my life.
86. It's too much work to lose this weight.
87. I will never be able to lose the weight.
88. I eat when I am overwhelmed with life.
89. I reward myself with my favorite foods.
90. I know my eating is out of control but…
91. I know overeating is irresponsible but…
92. I am not empowered to change my life.
93. My thinking is not positive or powerful.
94. I don't know how to create what I want.
95. I use food to make myself feel valuable.
96. I overeat to suppress and bury feelings.
97. I eat when I feel any emotional feelings.
98. I know overeating shortens my life but…
99. It's not okay/safe for me to lose weight.
100. Eating is not a conscious activity for me.

> The moment you commit and quit holding back, all sorts of unforeseen incidents, meetings and material assistance will rise up to help you. The simple act of commitment is a powerful magnet for help.
>
> Napoleon Hill

1. From the previous page, list the seven statements that you thought or felt applied to you:

1.

2.

3.

4.

5.

6.

7.

2. Select one of the statements from above and describe how it plays out in your life. Give an example or two. It is important to recognize and identify the pattern. Is there a trigger? How does it begin? How has it benefited you? How has it harmed you? For instance, is it impossible for you to succeed at dieting? Do you feel deprived then binge? Rather than "dieting," can you make a lifestyle change?

3. Tap the seven statements above. If more than seven applied, tap them as well.

4. As you were tapping, did you have any new thoughts, memories of the past surface, any additional insights, and/or an ah-ah awareness?

101. I am always thinking about food and eating.
102. My daily workout is not sacred or a priority.
103. I wait to do anything until I lose the weight.
104. I don't know how to lose the excess weight.
105. I overeat because I don't know what I need.
106. I know I overeat because I hate myself but...
107. My identity is that of an overweight person.
108. The only image I have of myself is being fat.
109. I am afraid to be happy, healthy, and strong.
110. I overeat when I don't want to feel anything.
111. I know I will fail at weight loss before I begin.
112. I don't know who I would be without my pain.
113. Eating is the only enjoyment I have in my life.
114. My behavior is not consistent with my desire.
115. I don't stop eating when I am satisfied or full.
116. I don't want to move out of my comfort zone.
117. I don't take the time to deal with my feelings.
118. I don't want to give up my old "safe" lifestyle.
119. I'm not consistent in my weight loss program.
120. I eat without thinking about what I am eating.
121. Being stressed leads to my being overweight.
122. Releasing resentment will not dissolve my fat.
123. The only control I have in my life is what I eat.
124. I always eat the food offered to me by others.
125. I don't know who I am without my food issues.

> Good health is more than just exercise and diet. It's really a point of view and a mental attitude you have about yourself.
>
> Angela Lansbury

1. From the previous page, list the seven statements that you thought or felt applied to you:

1.

2.

3.

4.

5.

6.

7.

2. Select one of the statements from above and describe how it plays out in your life. Give an example or two. It is important to recognize and identify the pattern. Is there a trigger? How does it begin? How has it benefited you? How has it harmed you? For instance, is your eating the only area of your life that is out of control? If not, what is the underlying issue(s)? Stress? Lack of self-confidence? Anger, fear, and/or apathy?

3. Tap the seven statements above. If more than seven applied, tap them as well.

4. As you were tapping, did you have any new thoughts, memories of the past surface, any additional insights, and/or an ah-ah awareness?

126. I sabotage my own weight loss efforts.
127. I use my excess weight to keep me safe.
128. I don't have the patience to lose weight.
129. I don't know who I would be if I was thin.
130. Food is synonymous with Mom and love.
131. Food is available when I feel abandoned.
132. I am always taking care of everyone else.
133. I'm tired of not caring about myself but...
134. I am not conscious of what or when I eat.
135. I know overeating diminishes my life but...
136. Food is available when I feel totally alone.
137. I stay busy so I don't have to think or feel.
138. I cannot successfully get past temptation.
139. I use food to satisfy my emotional hunger.
140. I will never be able to look the way I want.
141. I don't care that I'm not taking care of me.
142. I would feel selfish asking for what I need.
143. I continue to indulge all day once I blow it.
144. I know overeating robs me of energy but...
145. Life is synonymous with pain and struggle.
146. I know I shouldn't eat as much as I do but...
147. I feel depressed and guilty when I overeat.
148. I cannot imagine myself at my ideal weight.
149. Eating is the only pleasure I have in my life.
150. Feeling ugly leads to my being overweight.

> You cannot make footprints in the sands of time if you are sitting on your butt and who wants to make butt prints in the sand of time?
>
> Bob Moawad

1. From the previous page, list the seven statements that you thought or felt applied to you:

1.

2.

3.

4.

5.

6.

7.

2. Select one of the statements from above and describe how it plays out in your life. Give an example or two. It is important to recognize and identify the pattern. Is there a trigger? How does it begin? How has it benefited you? How has it harmed you? For instance, do you sabotage your weight loss program? Would you be able to maintain your ideal weight once you lost the excess weight? Do you sabotage other areas of your life?

3. Tap the seven statements above. If more than seven applied, tap them as well.

4. As you were tapping, did you have any new thoughts, memories of the past surface, any additional insights, and/or an ah-ah awareness?

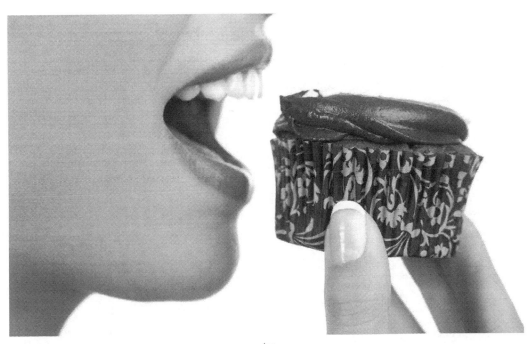

151. I eat when I feel rejected, unloved, and isolated.
152. The lack of peace leads to my being overweight.
153. I don't have the skills or tools to lose this weight.
154. I am afraid of being abandoned and/or rejected.
155. I know I am self-righteous about my weight but...
156. The stress to lose weight makes me gain weight.
157. I'm unwilling to make the time to exercise/move.
158. Feeling powerless leads to my being overweight.
159. My food choices are not consistent with my goal.
160. I'm not willing to lose weight in small increments.
161. Food fills me up when I feel empty and depleted.
162. Food is the one thing I allow myself to indulge in.
163. I overeat in an attempt to fulfill my unmet needs.
164. I don't know how to control how much food I eat.
165. I can't imagine my life without my food problems.
166. I will not feel happy until I weigh my ideal weight.
167. I sabotage my health program to remain invisible.
168. I'm not willing to move beyond the ache for food.
169. I overeat to comfort myself in stressful situations.
170. I stay heavy so that others feel secure around me.
171. Overeating is synonymous with comfort and calm.
172. The only thing I can control in my life is what I eat.
173. Overeating is synonymous with happiness and joy.
174. I know I am using food as a love replacement but...
175. I will not feel fulfilled until I weigh my ideal weight.

Every human being is the author of his own health or disease.

Buddha

1. From the previous page, list the seven statements that you thought or felt applied to you:

1.

2.

3.

4.

5.

6.

7.

2. Select one of the statements from above and describe how it plays out in your life. Give an example or two. It is important to recognize and identify the pattern. Is there a trigger? How does it begin? How has it benefited you? How has it harmed you? For instance, are you not willing to lose weight in small increments? Is it all-or-nothing in other areas of your life? Or is this a lack of patience or the inability to sustain a way of being for any length of time?

3. Tap the seven statements above. If more than seven applied, tap them as well.

4. As you were tapping, did you have any new thoughts, memories of the past surface, any additional insights, and/or an ah-ah awareness?

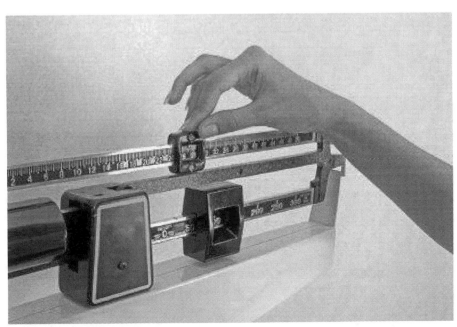

176. Life is synonymous with survival and hardship.
177. Disappointment leads to my emotional eating.
178. I know I overeat because I feel unlovable but...
179. Trying to lose weight puts me into overwhelm.
180. I put on a false front that everything is A-okay.
181. I allow others to sabotage my weight program.
182. I resent others telling me how and what to eat.
183. I don't know how to stop the emotional eating.
184. I eat out of habit and not because I am hungry.
185. Eating healthy food is emotionally unsatisfying.
186. I'm not able to concentrate on long-term goals.
187. It's not okay/safe for me to be my ideal weight.
188. I'm not willing to be my true and authentic self.
189. I live my life in constant regret and depression.
190. I eat when I want to avoid feeling my emotions.
191. I ignore the voice that tells me I am overeating.
192. I overeat to cover up feelings I cannot express.
193. Being frustrated leads to my being overweight.
194. Meals are anxious and unpleasant times for me.
195. Not liking myself leads to my being overweight.
196. Healthy food is like eating cardboard and grass.
197. Feeling hopeless leads to my being overweight.
198. My life would be different if I could lose weight.
199. I overeat due to problems and turmoil in my life.
200. I'm not deserving of good health and happiness.

> The biggest seller is cookbooks and the second is diet books - how not to eat what you've just learned how to cook.
>
> Andy Rooney

1. From the previous page, list the seven statements that you thought or felt applied to you:

1.

2.

3.

4.

5.

6.

7.

2. Select one of the statements from above and describe how it plays out in your life. Give an example or two. It is important to recognize and identify the pattern. Is there a trigger? How does it begin? How has it benefited you? How has it harmed you? For instance, are you not interested in healthy foods? If you don't take care of your body, where will you live?

3. Tap the seven statements above. If more than seven applied, tap them as well.

4. As you were tapping, did you have any new thoughts, memories of the past surface, any additional insights, and/or an ah-ah awareness?

201. I have given up hope that my life will ever improve.
202. I am not willing to ask for support/help/assistance.
203. I don't take small steps every day toward my goals.
204. Eating gives me something to do when I am bored.
205. I constantly beat myself up about my food choices.
206. My identift is tied up in my struggle to lose weight.
207. I will not feel satisfied until I weigh my ideal weight.
208. Food fills the emptiness of not having anyone close.
209. I will never be able to move beyond my food issues.
210. I reach for food when I want and need to feel loved.
211. I don't expect that I will ever weigh my ideal weight.
212. I know I should be more attentive to my health but...
213. I hold onto excess weight to numb myself from hurt.
214. I hold onto excess weight to numb myself from pain.
215. I know overeating is a symptom of other issues but...
216. I know overeating is an excuse for other things but...
217. I have a tendency to put people I love on a pedestal.
218. The quality of my life is limited by my excess weight.
219. I am not able to transform my relationship with food.
220. I know I am heavy to deter any sexual attention but...
221. I am emotionally distant from my needs and feelings.
222. I eat smaller portions when other people are around.
223. I'm not able to fill my emotional emptiness by myself.
224. I don't want others to know how much I weigh or eat.
225. I don't have the will to follow any plan to lose weight.

> Your biggest problem or difficulty today has been sent to you at this moment to teach you something you need to know to be happier and more successful in the future.
>
> Brian Tracy

1. From the previous page, list the seven statements that you thought or felt applied to you:

1.

2.

3.

4.

5.

6.

7.

2. Select one of the statements from above and describe how it plays out in your life. Give an example or two. It is important to recognize and identify the pattern. Is there a trigger? How does it begin? How has it benefited you? How has it harmed you? For instance, do you ever ask anyone to do anything for you? And the reason might be? They might say "no" and you will feel rejected? Or you don't need anyone and asking for help would be proof that you do?

3. Tap the seven statements above. If more than seven applied, tap them as well.

4. As you were tapping, did you have any new thoughts, memories of the past surface, any additional insights, and/or an ah-ah awareness?

226. I would rather be invisible than to weigh my ideal weight.
227. I am not willing to sacrifice now for a return in the future.
228. I know reducing the coffee will make me feel better but...
229. I don't know who I would be if I weighed my ideal weight.
230. Obsessing about food is a distraction from my real issues.
231. I know physical activity would help me to feel better but...
232. I have an addictive personality...overeating, overworking...
233. I overeat when I am craving affection and companionship.
234. Overeating is synonymous with reward and job well done.
235. I am always thinking about and struggling with my weight.
236. To maintain my ideal weight, I have to eat less than a bird.
237. I feel ashamed/guilty that I cannot lose weight on my own.
238. Overweight is synonymous with being invisible and hiding.
239. I feel life would be a lot different if I could lose this weight.
240. This excess weight has prevented me from so many things.
241. I know I would feel more relaxed if I cut out the sugar but...
242. I know a well-nourished body copes with stress better but...
243. The solution to permanent weight lose is impossible for me.
244. Those around me sabotage my health/weight loss program.
245. I know reducing the chocolate will make me feel better but...
246. I don't know how to fulfill my nurturing needs without eating.
247. I overeat when someone makes a comment about my weight.
249. Overeating is an attempt to avoid the emptiness I feel inside.
250. I know reducing the soft drinks will make me feel better but...

> A diet is the penalty we pay for exceeding the feed limit.
>
> Unknown

1. From the previous page, list the seven statements that you thought or felt applied to you:

1.

2.

3.

4.

5.

6.

7.

2. Select one of the statements from above and describe how it plays out in your life. Give an example or two. It is important to recognize and identify the pattern. Is there a trigger? How does it begin? How has it benefited you? How has it harmed you? For instance, would you rather be invisible than to weigh your ideal weight? What is your fear about being visible? Attention? Career advancement? New friendships and/or relationships? With any of these, your life would change. Would you rather your life stay the same?

3. Tap the seven statements above. If more than seven applied, tap them as well.

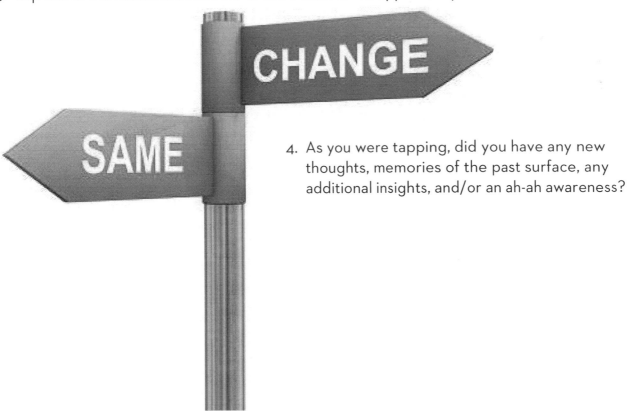

4. As you were tapping, did you have any new thoughts, memories of the past surface, any additional insights, and/or an ah-ah awareness?

251. I punish myself after I have eaten more than I should.

252. I'm not willing to totally change my life for the better.

253. I am always stressing about what and how much I eat.

254. Food is my only source of comfort, love, and security.

255. I overeat to compensate for what is missing in my life.

256. I overeat when I don't know how to handle a situation.

257. I cannot picture myself reaching my goal/ideal weight.

258. I am not willing to give up my favorite unhealthy foods.

259. I bribe myself with ___ to force myself to do a "should."

260. I'm not sure I would know who I am without the weight.

261. I become unraveled when someone judges me harshly.

262. Overeating is synonymous with depression and apathy.

263. I overeat when I am stressed, afraid, and overwhelmed.

264. I know others ignore me because I am overweight but...

265. The only way I know how to handle overwhelm is to eat.

266. I am intimidated by the possibility of others judging me.

267. I avoid _____ because of my weight.

268. I don't know what size portion of foods would fill me up.

269. I know I overeat because I don't care about myself but...

270. I blame others for my inability to reach my weight goals.

271. No one asks me to lunch when they know I am on a diet.

272. Anxiety and being worried lead to my being overweight.

273. Healthy food choices are not a natural way of life for me.

274. I am not willing to give up food as my coping mechanism.

275. I would have to constantly diet for permanent weight loss.

> When we set exciting worthwhile goals for ourselves, they work in two ways. We work on them and they work on us.
>
> Bob Moawad

1. From the previous page, list the seven statements that you thought or felt applied to you:

1.

2.

3.

4.

5.

6.

7.

2. Select one of the statements from above and describe how it plays out in your life. Give an example or two. It is important to recognize and identify the pattern. Is there a trigger? How does it begin? How has it benefited you? How has it harmed you? For instance, you cannot picture yourself reaching your goal/ideal weight. Is this because you don't want to be disappointed if you don't reach your goal? Do you think you would be setting yourself up for embarrassment if you did picture yourself at your ideal weight and then didn't reach your goal?

3. Tap the seven statements above. If more than seven applied, tap them as well.

4. As you were tapping, did you have any new thoughts, memories of the past surface, any additional insights, and/or an ah-ah awareness?

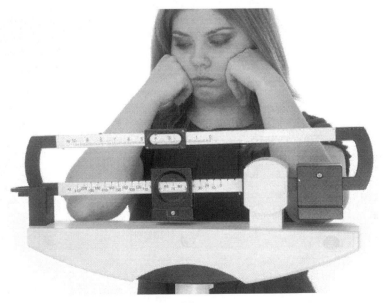

276. Knowing this is the best it gets leads to my being overweight.

277. I know I would feel more relaxed if I cut out the caffeine but...

278. I know stress has a profound effect on my physical health but...

279. I am not willing to give up temptation now for a future benefit.

280. I use food as a replacement for human contact and interaction.

281. I use food to distract me from feeling what I don't want to feel.

282. It makes me really uncomfortable to eat in front of thin people.

283. I am not committed to reaching or maintaining my ideal weight.

284. Overeating is synonymous with love and emotional satisfaction.

285. I am overwhelmed with the amount of fat/weight I have to lose.

286. I know the caffeine high will end with a crash in my energy but...

287. Fighting my weight is a diversion away from feeling my feelings.

288. I will never be able to love myself until I get over this food issue.

289. My only identity is that of a fat person, struggling to lose weight.

290. My compulsive eating is an attempt to avoid the absence of love.

291. I'm not willing to do the physical movement part of being healthy.

292. I'm not willing to take the time necessary to lose weight correctly.

293. Overeating is the only way I know how to make myself feel better.

294. I don't have the patience and/or time to lose weight the right way.

295. I'm not willing to do the work required to lose weight permanently.

296. I know eliminating sugar in my diet would make me feel better but...

297. I'm not able to motivate myself over the long haul to improve my health.

298. Overeating is synonymous with not being able to express and receive love.

299. I can't deal with the sexual attention I would get if I weighed my ideal weight.

300. Being healthy means hard work, struggle, loneliness, pressure, heartbreak, exposure, embarrassment, risk, and/or enduring pain. (Choose 3.)

> Brain cells come and brain cells go, but fat cells live forever.
>
> Unknown

1. From the previous page, list the seven statements that you thought or felt applied to you:

1.

2.

3.

4.

5.

6.

7.

2. Select one of the statements from above and describe how it plays out in your life. Give an example or two. It is important to recognize and identify the pattern. Is there a trigger? How does it begin? How has it benefited you? How has it harmed you? For instance, is your only identity that of a fat person, struggling to lose weight? Who would you be if you lost the weight? Is it easier to be a "weight loss failure" than a "weight loss success?" How well do you handle success?

3. Tap the seven statements above. If more than seven applied, tap them as well.

4. As you were tapping, did you have any new thoughts, memories of the past surface, any additional insights, and/or an ah-ah awareness?

BIBLIOGRAPHY

Britten, Rhonda, *Fearless Living, Live Without Excuses and Love Without Regret,* New York: Penguin Putnam, Inc., 2001.

Fuchs, Nan Kathryn, *Overcoming the Legacy of Overeating,* Los Angeles, CA.: Lowell House, 1999.

Gould, Roger, MD, *Shrink Yourself, Break Free From Emotional Eating Forever,* Hoboken, NJ: John wiley & Son, Inc., 2007.

Greene, Bob, *Get with the Program,* New York: Simon & Schuster, 2002.

Jampolsky, Lee, *Healing the Addictive Mind,* Berkeley, CA.: Celestial Arts, 1991.

Nakken, Craig, *The Addictive Personality,* Center City, MN.: Hazelden Foundation, 1996.

FOOD CRAVINGS

BREAD

CHOCOLATE

CRUNCHY FOODS

DAIRY

FATTY/FRIED FOODS

SALTY FOODS

SPICY FOODS

SWEETS

FOOD CRAVINGS

(Contributing Editor – Faith Shevlin)

Our food cravings are trying to tell us something and it's not about the foods.

* Craving sweets might indicate a lack of joy in our lives.
* Craving crunchy foods might be an indication of frustration we are feeling.
* Craving bread might be an attempt to fill emptiness in our lives.

Food Cravings are symptoms. They are not the issue. Food cravings are symptoms of deeper issues in our lives. They are indications of what we need to heal.

THE ONLY WAY TO TRULY END FOOD CRAVINGS IS TO HEAL THE CAUSE.

To heal our food cravings we have to recognize, acknowledge, address, desensitize, and/or delete the thoughts, emotions, and memories that propel us toward the foods we crave.

Healing begins with an awareness of our actions and an understanding of the triggers that lead to the action. Knowing the significance of our food cravings can provide insights into what we really are craving.

TO HEAL OUR FOOD CRAVINGS, WE NEED TO HEAL THE UNDERLYING CAUSE... OUR DYSFUNCTIONAL BELIEFS AND EMOTIONS.

BREAD

EMOTIONAL SIGNIFICANCE OF BREAD:

* An attempt to soothe tension, stress, and/or anxiety.
* Wanting to fill an inner emptiness.
* Looking for calm and comfort; reassurance.
* Feeling unsatisfied with life.
* A desire to ease pain.
* A desire to slow down.
* Calming and relaxing.

EFT TAPPING STATEMENTS FOR BREAD:

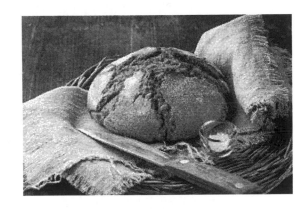

1. I like the feeling of being full.
2. I don't feel secure in the world.
3. My life is not satisfying or fulfilling.
4. I don't know how to find fulfillment.
5. I don't know what is missing in my life.
6. I crave bread when I am disappointed.
7. Eating bread fills the void I feel inside.
8. Bread is comforting when I feel lonely.
9. Bread is comforting when I feel empty.
10. I crave bread when I need reassurance.
11. I crave bread when I feel overwhelmed.
12. I can't get through a day without bread.
13. Bread is comforting when I am stressed.
14. There is something missing from my life.
15. I don't know what I need to feel fulfilled.
16. I can't keep up with everything in my life.
17. I crave bread when I want to be nurtured.
18. I crave bread when I want to be comforted.
19. I am totally addicted and attached to bread.
20. I crave bread when I am anxious and worried.
21. I eat bread when I feel overwhelmed with life.
22. I don't have the tools and skill to handle stress.
23. I want a guarantee that everything will work out.
24. I don't have the tools and skills to manage my anxiety.
25. There is not enough time to get everything accomplished.

Chocolate

Emotional Significance of Chocolate:

* Craving for love, intimacy, and/or romance.
* A need for calm.
* To lift one's mood, a "feel-good" boost.
* Looking for energy, passion, and/or excitement.
* Used as an anti-depressant.
* Unable to process sadness and grief.

EFT Tapping Statements for Chocolate:

1. My life lacks passion.
2. I have given up on love.
3. I crave love and romance.
4. I'm not in love with my life.
5. I fantasize about chocolate.
6. I need chocolate to do my life.
7. I crave chocolate when I am sad.
8. Eating chocolate soothes my pain.
9. My life lacks intimacy and romance.
10. I crave chocolates when I am lonely.
11. Chocolate makes everything better.
12. Chocolate makes everything A-okay.
13. I crave chocolate when I feel rejected.
14. I feel guilty when I indulge in chocolate.
15. I need chocolate to get through the day.
16. Chocolate gives me energy to do my life.
17. I crave chocolate when I don't feel loved.
18. The world melts away when I eat chocolate.
19. I need chocolate to handle the stresses of life.
20. I crave chocolate when I feel alone in the world.
21. Chocolate replaces the intimacy I lack in my life.
22. I crave chocolate to soothe my disappointments.
23. My day feels incomplete if I don't have chocolate.
24. I treat myself with chocolate when I want a reward.
25. Chocolate is one of my greatest source of pleasure.

CRUNCHY/CRISPY

EMOTIONAL SIGNIFICANCE OF CRUNCHY/CRISPY:

* An attempt to relieve anger, irritation, anxiety, and frustration.
* Stress relief.
* Lack "texture" in our lives.
* Longing for comfort and reassurance.
* Might be about anxiety, grief, sadness, depression, insecurity, regret, fear, self-doubt and/or shame.

EFT TAPPING STATEMENTS FOR CRUNCHY/CRISPY:

1. I am not my priority in life.
2. Crunching relieves my stress.
3. I get angry when I feel criticized.
4. I have a tendency to be impatient.
5. I am critical of myself and/or others.
6. I get impatient and/or annoyed easily.
7. I crave crunchy foods when I am angry.
8. I don't know how to heal my depression.
9. There is no one in my life to comfort me.

10. It is not okay or safe to express my anger.
11. I crave crunchy foods when I feel anxious.
12. I have a lot of anxiety, fear, and self-doubt.
13. I have a tendency to be anxious and worry.
14. I am angry I don't make my needs a priority.
15. I hide my anger, bitterness, and resentment.
16. I'm sad that this is the best my life will ever be.
17. I don't know what to do with the sadness I feel.
18. I crave crunchy foods when I need reassurance.
19. My life didn't turn out as I had thought it would.
20. I'm not sure I am living the life I want to be living.
21. I crave crunchy foods when I am feeling insecure.
22. I don't know how to heal my shame and self-doubt.
23. I crave crunchy foods when I feel I am being judged.
24. I am embarrassed when I am the center of attention.
25. I eat crunchy foods when someone finds fault with me.

Dairy
(Cheese, Ice Cream, Milk, Pudding, Creamy & Smooth)

Emotional Significance of Dairy:

* A craving for comfort.
* A yearning for being nurtured.
* Needing soothing.
* Looking for safety and security.
* To manage depression.
* To ease worry and anxiety.
* Feeling life is very tough and turbulent.
* Desire for life to be a little easier.

EFT Tapping Statements for Dairy:

1. Dairy soothes me.
2. Ice cream is comforting.
3. My life is constant chaos.
4. Dairy feels like mom's love.
5. Dairy eases my depression.
6. I don't take care of my needs.
7. I crave comfort and nurturing.
8. I crave dairy when I feel unsafe.
9. Life is very tough and turbulent.
10. I feel comforted when I eat dairy.
11. I crave dairy when I feel insecure.
12. I crave dairy when my life is tough.
13. I crave dairy when I feel burdened.
14. I crave dairy when I feel depressed.
15. I crave dairy when my life is chaotic.
16. I crave dairy when life is unbearable.
17. Dairy makes me feel safe and secure.
18. I crave dairy when I am in overwhelm.
19. I crave dairy when I feel overwhelmed.
20. I crave dairy when I wish life was easier.
21. I want someone else to take care of me.
22. I crave dairy when the going gets tough.
23. I crave dairy when my life lacks nurturing.
24. I crave dairy when I feel worried and anxious.
25. I am craving smoothness and softness in my life.

Fatty /Fried Foods

(Fried Foods, Ice Cream, High-fat Dairy)

Emotional Significance of Fatty Foods:

* Fills the emptiness.
* Feeling unsatisfied, unfulfilled, and/or empty.
* Yearning for the richness of life.
* A lack of inspiration in life.
* Lacking self-esteem and self-worth.
* Desire to accept our own authenticity.

EFT Tapping Statements for Fatty/Fried Foods:

1. My life lacks meaning.
2. My life lacks "richness."
3. I play my life small and safe.
4. My life will never be fulfilling.
5. It is difficult to accept myself.
6. I yearn for the richness of life.
7. My self-esteem is non-existent.
8. My desires are out of my reach.
9. My life is unfulfilling and empty.
10. My needs will never be fulfilled.
11. I have nothing important to offer.
12. I don't know what would fulfill me.
13. I eat fried foods when I feel unworthy.
14. I lack inspiration to live a meaningful life.
15. I don't know how to overcome my apathy.
16. I eat fatty foods when my life feels empty.
17. I eat fatty foods when I want to escape life.
18. It is hopeless I will ever achieve my desires.
19. I will never accomplish anything worthwhile.
20. I don't have the courage to pursue my dreams.
21. I don't know how to heal my emotional wounds.
22. I don't have the courage to be my authentic self.
23. I crave fatty/fried foods when I feel I have no worth.
24. I crave fatty/fried foods when I feel less than others.
25. I crave fatty/fried foods when I yearn for the richness of life.

Salty Foods

NCE OF SALTY:

ounding, stability, and/or security.
n our lives.
* A need for down time and relaxation.
* "Salt of the earth."
* Might be about stress, anger, anxiety.
* Desire to heal emotional stagnation.
* Desire to let go of stress.
* Desire to release emotions.

EFT TAPPING STATEMENTS FOR SALTY:

1. My comfort zone is a rut.
2. I never have time to just be.
3. I am not grounded or stable.
4. I yearn for stability in my life.
5. I don't know how to handle stress.
6. My life lacks stability and security.
7. I don't know how to live in the flow.
8. I am only safe when my life is stable.
9. It is not comfortable for me to relax.
10. I crave salty foods when I am stressed.
11. I crave salty foods when I feel anxious.
12. I am anxious when my life lacks security.
13. I am fearful of moving into the unknown.
14. I am unable to deal with emotional stress.
15. I blame myself for all the wrong in my life.
16. I am safe only when I ignore my emotions.
17. It not okay or safe to express my emotions.
18. I crave salty foods when I feel ungrounded.
19. I don't know how to go with the flow of life.
20. I don't know how to heal my emotional pain.
21. I crave salty food when life is overwhelming.
22. I don't know how to create stability in my life.
23. I don't know how to replenish what I have lost.
24. I can't move forward in my life without stability.
25. I crave salty food when I feel life is out of control.

SPICY FOODS

EMOTIONAL SIGNIFICANCE OF SPICY:

* A craving and drive for intensity and excitement.
* Searching for passion.
* Response to boredom.
* Wanting more adventure.
* Looking for action in our lives.
* Wanting to "spice up" our life.
* Wanting more variety in our life.
* Wanting more in life and out of life.

EFT TAPPING STATEMENTS FOR SPICY:

1. I crave excitement.
2. I am bored with my life.
3. My life lacks excitement.
4. My life is dull and mundane.
5. I crave more spice in my life.
6. I crave more variety in my life.
7. I am stuck in a monotonous rut.
8. My life is boring and unexciting.
9. I have nothing to look forward to.
10. I do the same thing day after day.
11. I feel alive when I eat spicy foods.
12. I crave more excitement in my life.
13. I crave spicy food when I am bored.
14. I want more of everything in my life.
15. I have given up on adventure and fun.
16. I'm frustrated that my life is so boring.
17. My passions are nowhere to be found.
18. I don't deserve to have the life I desire.
19. My dreams are too grand to be fulfilled.
20. I crave the excitement that risks provide.
21. Eating spicy foods adds variety to my life.
22. Eating spicy foods adds "spice" to my life.
23. I crave spicy food when I crave excitement.
24. Eating spicy foods spices up my boring life.
25. I thought life would be more exciting than it is.

SWEETS
(CANDY, DONUTS, PASTRIES, CAKE, COOKIES, ICE CREAM)

EMOTIONAL SIGNIFICANCE OF SWEETS:

* A craving for sweetness in life.
* A lack of joy in life.
* Wanting a reward.
* Seeking pleasure.
* Don't feel "sweet" enough.
* Needing a boost of energy.
* Feeling exhausted.

* A lack of self-care and "me" time.
* Unable to process sadness and grief.
* A desire to avoid disappointment.
* Feeling that change and healing are hopeless.
* Cookies are hugs, pleasure, and reassurance.
* Candy is a sweet pick-me-up and reward.

EFT TAPPING STATEMENTS FOR SWEETS:

1. I am not sweet enough.
2. My life lacks sweetness.
3. My joy is nowhere to be found.
4. Sweets get me through the day.
5. I don't create enough "me" time.
6. I fantasize about sweets all day long.
7. Sweets lift me up when I am dragging.
8. I could eat endless amounts of sweets.
9. I deserve a sweet reward for all that I do.

10. I crave sweets when I want to reward myself.
11. I don't know how to face my sadness and hurt.
12. I don't know how to heal my sadness and hurt.
13. I feel deprived if I don't have something sweet.
14. I eat sweets when I am feeling sorry for myself.
15. It is hopeless that I will ever have the life I want.
16. I indulge in sweets to numb my disappointments.
17. My day is incomplete if I don't have anything sweet.
18. I don't have enough energy to accomplish all my goals.
19. I acknowledge my accomplishments with a sweet treat.
20. Eating sweets is the only way I can get through the day.
21. It is hopeless that I will ever resolve my hurt and sadness.
22. There isn't enough time in the day for my needs to be met.
23. It is hopeless that my life will be any different than it is now.
24. The only thing I have to look forward to is my sweet reward.
25. It feels like something is missing if I don't have a sweet treat.

ANGER

ANGER

Anger and frustration are natural emotions. Anger is not in itself right or wrong, healthy or unhealthy, appropriate or inappropriate. It is the **expression** of anger that makes it right or wrong, healthy or unhealthy, appropriate or inappropriate. Unhealthy anger is when anger is directed toward another for the purpose of being hurtful and to do harm. Wrong and inappropriate anger is when anger is violent and is used to punish, intimidate, control, and manipulate.

Anger that is repressed and aggressive is unhealthy anger. It is unhealthy to stuff, ignore, and/or pretend the anger does not exist.

* RESENTMENT is unexpressed anger.

* PASSIVE-AGGRESSIVE ANGER is anger meant to inflict pain.

* RAGE is abusive anger filled with feelings of fear, sadness, shame, inadequacy, guilt, and/or loss.

*DEPRESSION is anger we think we would get in trouble for having, thus depress the anger.

*GUILT is anger we don't feel we have a right to have.

* APATHY is suppressed anger.

*WORRY is anticipated anger.

*ANXIETY is a combination of four things: UNIDENTIFIED ANGER, HURT, FEAR, AND SELF-PITY.

We expect error, rejection, humiliation, and actually start to anticipate it.

Unresolved anger can lead to serious physical and mental health problems, such as heart disease, stroke, depression, and anxiety.

Suppressed anger can lead to depression, violence, or obsession. Old, suppressed anger can emerge at any time in response to a present situation. The response may be inappropriate, reactive, and might have nothing to do with the present situation.

There is always something more that feeds the anger than what is observed on the surface. Angry people may appear strong, willful, or certain, but be assured that beneath the veneer there is fear, loneliness, insecurity, and pain.

Les Carter

Mis-belief Tapping Statements for Anger

1. My life is empty.
2. My life is pathetic.
3. Anger rules my life.
4. Anger is the enemy.
5. My health is crappy.
6. I am full of self-hate.
7. I eat when I am hurt.
8. I eat when I am angry.
9. My anger controls me.
10. Life is hostile and cruel.
11. I try to never get angry.
12. Anger is my only defense.
13. I am a dedicated pessimist.
14. I'm an expert at self-abuse.
15. I act in ugly and mean ways.
16. I have no right to get angry.
17. I hate myself for overeating.
18. I'm an expert at self-neglect.
19. I use food to soothe my pain.
20. I am not willing to feel anger.
21. I am disgusted with my body.
22. I often feel inferior to others.
23. I cover my shame with anger.
24. I am not entitled to my anger.
25. My anger is self-preservation.

Anger on David Hawkins' Map of Consciousness calibrates at 150. Courage is 200. It does not take courage to get angry. It does take courage to climb up to courage to heal the anger.

Tessa Cason

1. From the previous page, list the seven statements that you thought or felt applied to you:

1.

2.

3.

4.

5.

6.

7.

2. Select one of the statements from above and describe how it plays out in your life. Give an example or two. It is important to recognize and identify the pattern. Is there a trigger? How does it begin? How has it benefited you? How has it harmed you? For instance, are you a dedicated pessimist? Is it easier to be a pessimist so that if things don't work out you can say, "I knew it." Or are you a dedicated pessimist because you ran out of hope a long time ago?

3. Tap the seven statements above. If more than seven applied, tap them as well.

4. As you were tapping, did you have any new thoughts, memories of the past surface, any additional insights, and/or an ah-ah awareness?

26. I eat when others judge me harshly.
27. I feel guilty after I blow up in anger.
28. I am angry no one values who I am.
29. I get angry at myself after I overeat.
30. I am hurt when someone insults me.
31. I am not willing to give up my anger.
32. I feel angry and sick when I overeat.
33. I am angry at, and punishing, myself.
34. My anger is too powerful to control.
35. I'm too gullible when I am optimistic.
36. I judge others and/or myself harshly.
37. When I am angry, I act before I think.
38. I am angry that I sabotage my health.
39. It seems I am angry most of the time.
40. I hang onto my anger for a long time.
41. I don't want to admit how angry I get.
42. I feel used and manipulated by others.
43. It is not okay/safe for me to get angry.
44. It is doubtful I can turn my life around.
45. I am angry that I yo-yo with my weight.
46. I am always on guard to defend myself.
47. Other people's anger makes me angry.
48. Others will reject me when I get angry.
49. I refuse to let go of my anger and hate.
50. I don't know how to let go of my anger.

> Anger is our emotional response, our button being pushed, our issue, and thus, our responsibility to heal.
>
> Tessa Cason

1. From the previous page, list the seven statements that you thought or felt applied to you:

1.

2.

3.

4.

5.

6.

7.

2. Select one of the statements from above and describe how it plays out in your life. Give an example or two. It is important to recognize and identify the pattern. Is there a trigger? How does it begin? How has it benefited you? How has it harmed you? For instance, are you willing to give up your anger? Is it easier to stay angry than to deal with the anger? Do you know how to let your anger go? Or does your power come from being angry?

3. Tap the seven statements above. If more than seven applied, tap them as well.

4. As you were tapping, did you have any new thoughts, memories of the past surface, any additional insights, and/or an ah-ha awareness?

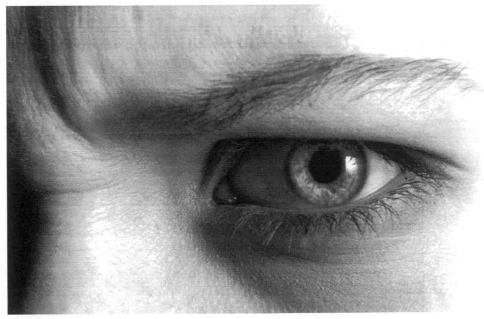

51. I allow others to put me down.
52. My anger comes on really fast.
53. Loving people don't get angry.
54. I am angry because I am angry.
55. I am a depressed, bitter grump.
56. I blame my problems on others.
57. It is not okay/safe to feel anger.
58. I tell others exactly what I think.
59. I am angry that I am not enough.
60. I am angry that my life is not fun.
61. I make others hurt for loving me.
62. I eat when I have been criticized.
63. I am full of anger, rage, and hate.
64. I am angry that I emotionally eat.
65. I feel guilty that I am overweight.
66. I hold grudges and don't forgive.
67. Anger is to be avoided at all cost.
68. Life is one problem after another.
69. I don't have any right to be angry.
70. I am condemning and judgmental.
71. I don't tell others when I feel hurt.
72. Criticism bothers me a great deal.
73. The world is full of hate and scorn.
74. I am angry that I don't love myself.
75. I blame my problems on my weight.

Headstone on a grave: "Here lies the angriest person in the world. He's probably complaining to the devil that hell is to hot!" How do you want to be remembered?

Tessa Cason

1. From the previous page, list the seven statements that you thought or felt applied to you:

1.

2.

3.

4.

5.

6.

7.

2. Select one of the statements from above and describe how it plays out in your life. Give an example or two. It is important to recognize and identify the pattern. Is there a trigger? How does it begin? How has it benefited you? How has it harmed you? For instance, do you blame your problems on others? If you do, then you never have to change. Is change the issue? You don't know how to change? When we blame and complain we don't have to look at ourselves or our issues.

3. Tap the seven statements above. If more than seven applied, tap them as well.

4. As you were tapping, did you have any new thoughts, memories of the past surface, any additional insights, and/or an ah-ah awareness?

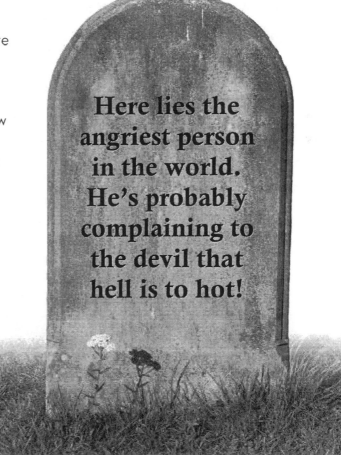

Here lies the angriest person in the world. He's probably complaining to the devil that hell is to hot!

76. It is not okay or safe to express my anger.
77. I'm not willing to let go of my resentment.
78. It is not okay/safe for me to be optimistic.
79. I get very angry when people criticize me.
80. I keep people at a safe distance by raging.
81. I blame others for what is wrong in my life.
82. I am afraid of anger and avoid it at all cost.
83. I don't know how to heal my hurt and pain.
84. I am so tired of being nice I could explode.
85. I stuff my feelings instead of healing them.
86. I'm not willing to give up my comfort food.
87. I get depressed when someone insults me.
88. I am angry that I need others to feel loved.
89. I use anger to avoid other issues in my life.
90. I am stubborn, immovable, and demanding.
91. I get really nervous when others are angry.
92. I feel guilty when I do fun things for myself.
93. I am angry that I depend on others for love.
94. I am angry that I sabotage myself with food.
95. I use anger to avoid emotional connections.
96. My anger will never stop once I get started.
97. I always have a restless feeling inside of me.
98. I don't have the wisdom to handle my anger.
99. I am angry that I can't eat like everyone else.
100. I'm tired of dieting and always having to diet.

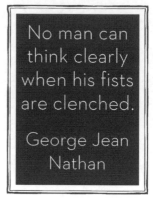

No man can think clearly when his fists are clenched.

George Jean Nathan

1. From the previous page, list the seven statements that you thought or felt applied to you:

1.

2.

3.

4.

5.

6.

7.

2. Select one of the statements from above and describe how it plays out in your life. Give an example or two. It is important to recognize and identify the pattern. Is there a trigger? How does it begin? How has it benefited you? How has it harmed you? For instance, do you stuff your feelings instead of healing them? Do you stuff yourself until you are beyond full? What would happen if you felt your feelings? Would you be overwhelmed if you felt your feelings?

3. Tap the seven statements above. If more than seven applied, tap them as well.

4. As you were tapping, did you have any new thoughts, memories of the past surface, any additional insights, and/or an ah-ah awareness?

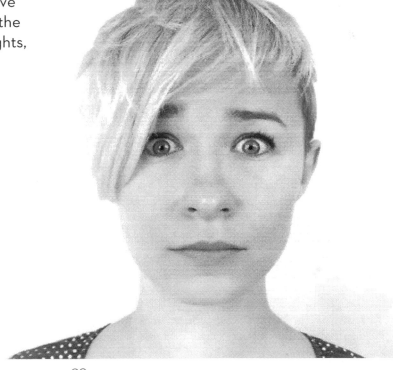

101. I keep old wounds bleeding and from healing.
102. My expectations for myself are unreasonable.
103. I'm tired of wearing clothes to hide my shape.
104. Nothing good is ever going to happen for me.
105. I am angry that to be healthy I have to be thin.
106. I handle my problems poorly when I am angry.
107. I would rather comply than face confrontation.
108. I don't know how to move forward with my life.
109. I am angry that I gain weight just by breathing.
110. It is not okay/safe for me to express my anger.
111. I am cynical, critical, and/or negative about life.
112. I feel guilty and irresponsible when I get angry.
113. I am angry I am holding onto this extra weight.
114. Outer circumstances control my inner feelings.
115. The only time I am powerful is when I am angry.
116. I am angry that to be healthy I have to exercise.
117. My terror will always overpower my confidence.
118. I feel stupid and out of control when I get angry.
119. Sometimes it feels like people are out to get me.
120. I am angry that I allow myself to be manipulated.
121. I don't know what to do with anger when I feel it.
122. I overeat when I am anticipating disappointment.
123. I'm tired of the stares I get for being overweight.
124. I get angry if anyone comments about my weight.
125. I'm tired of making excuses for being overweight.

> Blowing out another's candle will not make yours shine brighter.
>
> Unknown

1. From the previous page, list the seven statements that you thought or felt applied to you:

1.

2.

3.

4.

5.

6.

7.

2. Select one of the statements from above and describe how it plays out in your life. Give an example or two. It is important to recognize and identify the pattern. Is there a trigger? How does it begin? How has it benefited you? How has it harmed you? For instance, do you handle problems poorly because you are angry or are you angry because you handle problems poorly? Are you angry because you are confused, anxious, and unsure? Do you have the tools and skills to handle problems, to find solutions?

3. Tap the seven statements above. If more than seven applied, tap them as well.

4. As you were tapping, did you have any new thoughts, memories of the past surface, any additional insights, and/or an ah-ah awareness?

126. I am totally hopeless and full of despair.
127. I deny that I am angry when I am angry.
128. Others take advantage of my optimism.
129. I get depressed when I lose my temper.
130. I have no idea how to eat to be healthy.
131. I turn little annoyances into huge crisis.
132. I use humor to avoid facing my feelings.
133. I will lose total control when I get angry.
134. My anger is unexpected and unplanned.
135. I get angry if anyone ever questions me.
136. I do destructive things when I am angry.
137. I carry grudges for long periods of time.
138. Life owes me more than it has given me.
139. I hate that others stare at me when I eat.
140. I overeat when others find fault with me.
141. I am angry at other people's insensitivity.
142. I feel insulted and impatient with people.
143. I get angry when I feel bad about myself.
144. It is not okay or safe for me to get angry.
145. I allow anger to destroy my relationships.
146. I am intimidated by other people's anger.
147. I yell back at people that are angry at me.
148. I get angry when I have to defend myself.
149. I am easily provoked and short-tempered.
150. I use anger to push people out of my life.

> Let us not look back in anger or forward in fear, but around in awareness.
> James Thurber

1. From the previous page, list the seven statements that you thought or felt applied to you:

1.

2.

3.

4.

5.

6.

7.

2. Select one of the statements from above and describe how it plays out in your life. Give an example or two. It is important to recognize and identify the pattern. Is there a trigger? How does it begin? How has it benefited you? How has it harmed you? For instance, do you feel insulted and impatient with people? If so, is this about them or you? Is this about your lack of relationship skills? Or maybe others don't value and appreciate you as you think you should be? Do you allow anger to destroy your relationships? Or are your relationships destroyed because you don't know how to do relationships and thus, blame it on anger?

3. Tap the seven statements above. If more than seven applied, tap them as well.

4. As you were tapping, did you have any new thoughts, memories of the past surface, any additional insights, and/or an ah-ah awareness?

151. I am angry that I will never be able to lose weight.
152. I use food to change my focus away from my pain.
153. I don't have the tools to deal with disappointment.
154. I am not willing to recognize and accept my anger.
155. I have given up hope that my life will ever improve.
156. I don't have the tools and skills to handle my anger.
157. I am angry that I am ignored because of my weight.
158. I use my history to justify my irresponsible behavior.
159. I am angry and frustrated having to please everyone.
160. I am angry that I use food as a reward if I lose weight.
161. I am angry that all the dieting I do only to gain it back.
162. Being used and abused leads to my being overweight.
163. I use sarcasm instead of confronting someone directly.
164. I know I am playing victim and wallowing in my self-pity.
165. I overeat to mask my feelings of sadness, fear, and anger.
166. I use rage to cover my shame and feelings of inadequacy.
167. I use humor to keep others from knowing how I really feel.
168. I am angry that I eat well and the weight does not come off.
169. I am angry that others don't support my effects to lose weigh.
170. I hold onto excess weight to numb myself from disappointment.
171. I am angry that others judge me based on my outer appearance.
172. I am angry that I take care of my health and I am still overweight.
173. I am angry that others don't take me seriously because of my weight.
174. I am angry that people make judgments about me because of my weight.
175. I am angry that I have to deprive myself of the foods I love to lose weight.

He who angers you conquers you.

Elizabeth Kenny

1. From the previous page, list the seven statements that you thought or felt applied to you:

1.

2.

3.

4.

5.

6.

7.

2. Select one of the statements from above and describe how it plays out in your life. Give an example or two. It is important to recognize and identify the pattern. Is there a trigger? How does it begin? How has it benefited you? How has it harmed you? For instance, are you angry that you are ignored because of your weight? Who are you angry at and for what? Are you angry at someone else's judgement of you? Are you angry at yourself that you have given them a reason to judge you? Or is it anger at yourself for putting you in a vulnerable position in which you are judged by your outer appearance?

3. Tap the seven statements above. If more than seven applied, tap them as well.

4. As you were tapping, did you have any new thoughts, memories of the past surface, any additional insights, and/or an ah-ah awareness?

Bibliography

Borysenko, Joan, *Guilt is the Teacher Love is the Lesson,* NY: Warner Books, 1990.

Carter, Les, *Getting the Best of your Anger,* Grand Rapids, MI: Baker Book House Company, 1983.

Carter, Les, *The Anger Trap: Free Yourself from the Frustrations that Sabotage Your Life* NJ: Jossey-Bass, 2004.

Hanh, Thich Nhat, *Anger: Wisdom for Cooling the Flames,* NY: Riverhead Trade, 2002.

Lerner, Harriet, *The Dance of Anger: A Woman's Guide to Changing the Patterns of Intimate Relationships*, NY: Harper Paperbacks, 2005.

Potter-Efron, Ron & Pat Potter-Efron, *Letting Go of Anger,* Oakland, CA.: New Harbinger Publications, Inc., 1995.

Potter-Efron, Ronald T. & Patricia S. Potter-Efron, *Letting Go of Anger: The Eleven Most Common Anger Styles And What to Do About Them ,* Oakland, CA.: New Harbinger Publications, Inc., 2006.

GRIEF

GRIEF

Grief is more than sadness. It is more than unhappiness. Grief is a loss. Something of value is gone. Grief is an intense loss that breaks our heart. Loss can be the death of a loved one, a way of life, a job, a marriage, one's own imminent death. Grief is real.

Grief has many faces. Grief can show up as:

* Pain
* Hurt
* Shame
* Apathy
* Regret
* Depression
* Loneliness
* Hopelessness

* Disillusionment
* Disappointment
* Feeling unloved
* Feeling rejected
* Shattered dreams
* Feeling overwhelmed
* Feeling we don't belong
* Feeling that life and our life is meaningless

Over time, unhealed grief becomes anger, blame, resentment, righteousness, and/or remorse. We become someone we are not. It takes courage to move through the grief and all the emotions buried deep within. The depth of our pain is an indication the importance and significance something has for us.

* How has your life been limited by your weight? A romantic relationship? A job and/or a promotion at work?

* Has your weight prevented you from living the life you thought you would be living?

* Has your weight prevented you from having the marriage and/or family you desired?

* Do you avoid doing specific activity because of your weight?

* Do you have the energy needed to fulfill your wished?

WHAT HAVE YOU LOST AS A RESULT OF THE EXCESS WEIGHT YOU CARRY AROUND DAY AFTER DAY AFTER DAY?

Elisabeth Kubler-Ross developed five states of grief. These states are not sequential, they may coexist with other states, be completely skipped, occur intermittently, or repeat themselves. She believed that grief was a continuously evolving process that offers potential for growth. States are: Denial, Anger, Bargaining, Depression, and Acceptance.

The Grand Canyon was not punished by windstorms over hundreds of years. In fact, it was created by them. We are a creation with the unbelievable power to weather life's toughest storms. If someone had tried to shield the Grand Canyon from the windstorm, we would never have the beauty of its carvings.

Elisabeth Kubler-Ross and David

Mis-belief Tapping Statements for Grief/Sadness

1. I mourn the past.
2. I am stuck in grief.
3. I hold onto my grief.
4. I eat when I feel sad.
5. Life is tragic and dark.
6. My pain will never end.
7. I eat when I feel lonely.
8. I don't accept my grief.
9. It is not okay to be sad.
10. The tears seem endless.
11. I feel physically drained.
12. I am lost in a depression.
13. I don't belong anywhere.
14. I don't want to feel grief.
15. Nothing ever excites me.
16. Sorrow is the price of life.
17. I can't get on with my life.
18. My grief is destroying me.
19. I feel sad, hurt, and lonely.
20. It's one loss after another.
21. I am disillusioned with life.
22. I'm just existing, not living.
23. I don't accept my feelings.
24. I don't know how to grieve.
25. Grief is a sign of weakness.

> Hiding in my room, safe within my womb, I touch no one and no one touches me. I am a rock, I am an island. And a rock feels no pain and an island never cries.
>
> Paul Simon from song *I Am a Rock*

1. From the previous page, list the seven statements that you thought or felt applied to you:

1.

2.

3.

4.

5.

6.

7.

2. Select one of the statements from above and describe how it plays out in your life. Give an example or two. It is important to recognize and identify the pattern. Is there a trigger? How does it begin? How has it benefited you? How has it harmed you? For instance, do you hold onto your grief? Does living scare you? Will more be asked and expected of you if you were happy? Do you think you would fail if more was asked of you?

3. Tap the seven statements above. If more than seven applied, tap them as well.

4. As you were tapping, did you have any new thoughts, memories of the past surface, any additional insights, and/or an ah-ah awareness?

26. I don't know how to heal my grief.
27. I will never move through my pain.
28. I am too depressed to lose weight.
29. I use food to soothe my loneliness.
30. I feel disconnected from everyone.
31. I eat when I feel life is meaningless.
32. I feel overwhelmed and disoriented.
33. I am not important and don't matter.
34. I am sad that I am invisible to others.
35. I eat when everything feels hopeless.
36. My emotional wounds will never heal.
37. I seem to do everything at half speed.
38. I don't have the tools to heal my grief.
39. It is important that I suppress my grief.
40. It is difficult to make it through the day.
41. There is no point in waking up each day.
42. I don't know how to heal what is broken.
43. I'm constantly preoccupied with my loss.
44. I have allowed my weight to limit my life.
45. I have constant feelings of hopelessness.
46. I eat when I don't feel I belong anywhere.
47. I am sad that diet after diet has failed me.
48. I don't have the energy to get out of bed.
49. I don't know what loving myself looks like.
50. I am disappointed every time I am hopeful.

> Grief is like the ocean. It comes on waves ebbing and flowing. Sometimes the water is calm and sometimes it is overwhelming. All we can do is learn to swim.
>
> Vicki Harrison

1. From the previous page, list the seven statements that you thought or felt applied to you:

1.

2.

3.

4.

5.

6.

7.

2. Select one of the statements from above and describe how it plays out in your life. Give an example or two. It is important to recognize and identify the pattern. Is there a trigger? How does it begin? How has it benefited you? How has it harmed you? For instance, do you feel disconnected from everyone? Is it easier to disconnect than learn relationship skills? Are you convinced that if you were in a relationship you would be rejected?

3. Tap the seven statements above. If more than seven applied, tap them as well.

4. As you were tapping, did you have any new thoughts, memories of the past surface, any additional insights, and/or an ah-ah awareness?

51. My grief will go on forever.

52. I am sad that my life is a lie.

53. I am sad by what I have lost.

54. I am sad I fail diet after diet.

55. I don't want to feel the pain.

56. I am apathetic about my life.

57. I yearn for what I don't have.

58. I use food to soothe my hurt.

59. I can't move past devastation.

60. It is not safe to be vulnerable.

61. I'm having difficulty forgiving.

62. I'm having difficulty letting go.

63. I'm having difficulty accepting.

64. I don't know how to start anew.

65. My dreams have been crushed.

66. I use food to numb my sadness.

67. I lack the tools to heal my grief.

68. I feel as if I am coming unglued.

69. I live my life with the brakes on.

70. I eat when I feel life is hopeless.

71. I have a constant sense of doom.

72. I feel lost, unable to find my way.

73. My desires will never be fulfilled.

74. I eat when I feel no one loves me.

75. I am saddened by my past choices.

> Having experienced, struggled with, and come to terms with my own particular share of 'necessary losses' over the years, I've come to realize that those losses have taught me some of life's most valuable lessons.
>
> Marty Tousley

1. From the previous page, list the seven statements that you thought or felt applied to you:

1.

2.

3.

4.

5.

6.

7.

2. Select one of the statements from above and describe how it plays out in your life. Give an example or two. It is important to recognize and identify the pattern. Is there a trigger? How does it begin? How has it benefited you? How has it harmed you? For instance, have your dreams been crushed? What are you doing to create new dreams? Or it is easier to play victim and to feel sorry for yourself? Are you waiting for a guarantee before you begin again?

3. Tap the seven statements above. If more than seven applied, tap them as well.

4. As you were tapping, did you have any new thoughts, memories of the past surface, any additional insights, and/or an ah-ah awareness?

76. I'm lost in a maze of "if only" and "what if" statements.
77. Food is always there when there is no one to hold me.
78. I am sad that magic and miracles don't happen for me.
79. The only way I know how to handle loneliness is to eat.
80. I'm having difficulty letting go of my sadness and grief.
81. I cannot recover after my dreams have been shattered.
82. It's not okay/safe to nurture myself the way I would like.
83. I am sad that others can't see pass the weight to see me.
84. Food is always there when there is no one to comfort me.
85. I am sad that I don't have the energy to do exciting things.
86. I'm sad that I don't have the courage to pursue my dreams.
87. The only way I know how to handle the depression is to eat.
88. I am sad that I have not been successful at losing the weight.
89. It is hopeless that I will ever be able to lose the excess weight.
90. I am sad that my life has been diminished by the excess weight.
91. I would be overwhelmed with grief if I allowed myself to grieve.
92. I am sad that I don't have the willpower needed to lose the weight.
93. I am embarrassed by the excess weight I carry everywhere with me.
94. I'm sad that no one takes me seriously because of my excess weight.
95. My weight has prevented me from _____.
96. My weight has prevented me from doing _____.
97. I am sad that my weight has prevented me from having my hearts desires.
98. I am sad that I haven't live the life I wanted because of this excess weight.
99. My weight has prevented me from having what I thought I would have had.
100. My weight has prevented me from living the life I thought I would have lived.

> People are lonely because they build walls instead of bridges.
>
> J. F. Newton

1. From the previous page, list the seven statements that you thought or felt applied to you:

1.

2.

3.

4.

5.

6.

7.

2. Select one of the statements from above and describe how it plays out in your life. Give an example or two. It is important to recognize and identify the pattern. Is there a trigger? How does it begin? How has it benefited you? How has it harmed you? For instance, are you embarrassed by the excess weight you carry everywhere with you? Embarrassment is actually anger. Is it okay to be angry at yourself? We don't take action until we are finally fed up? Embarrassment must not be enough for you to take action. If not, what would be?

3. Tap the seven statements above. If more than seven applied, tap them as well.

4. As you were tapping, did you have any new thoughts, memories of the past surface, any additional insights, and/or an ah-ah awareness?

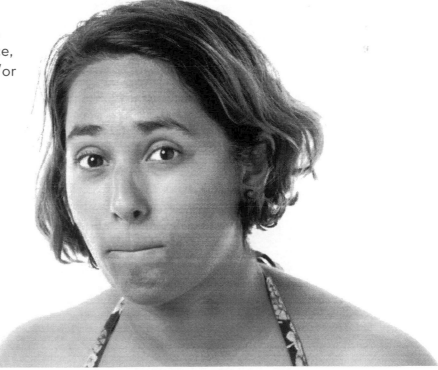

101. I am sad that my weight has limited my life.
102. I don't know how to move beyond my grief.
103. Life seems meaningless and overwhelming.
104. It seems I have been grieving my whole life.
105. I have missed out so much on life and living.
106. I'm overwhelmed with a sense of emptiness.
107. I feel like I'm in a dark room with no way out.
108. I am lost and don't know how to find my way.
109. I will never be able to release all my sadness.
110. I can't stop thinking about what I didn't have.
111. I will never be able to move beyond my grief.
112. I don't know who I would be without my grief.
113. I have not been able to move beyond my grief.
114. I live my life in a state of mourning for the past.
115. I'm overwhelmed with a sense of hopelessness.
116. Grief and sadness are my burden to carry in life.
117. I'm having difficulty finding meaning in anything.
118. I have a constant sense of emptiness and despair.
119. I fear rejection and not being accepted by others.
120. I've been knocked down and don't care if I get up.
121. I am sad that I don't have the energy to do my life.
122. It's hopeless that I will ever weigh my ideal weight.
123. I avoid disappointment by not getting my hopes up.
124. I am sad that others only see my weight and not me.
125. My grief keeps me from moving forward with my life.

> Even a happy life cannot be without a measure of darkness and the word happiness would lose its meaning if it were not balanced by sadness.
>
> Carl Jung

1. From the previous page, list the seven statements that you thought or felt applied to you:

1.

2.

3.

4.

5.

6.

7.

2. Select one of the statements from above and describe how it plays out in your life. Give an example or two. It is important to recognize and identify the pattern. Is there a trigger? How does it begin? How has it benefited you? How has it harmed you? For instance, are you having difficulty finding meaning in anything? Little action takes place when we are confused. Is the issue about "taking action" or the "nothing interest me?" Or are you lost in grief?

3. Tap the seven statements above. If more than seven applied, tap them as well.

4. As you were tapping, did you have any new thoughts, memories of the past surface, any additional insights, and/or an ah-ah awareness?

BIBLIOGRAPHY

Beattie, Melody, *The Grief Club, The Secret of Getting Through All Kinds of Change,* Center City, MN.: Hazelden, 2006.

Becvar, Dorothy S., *In The Presence of Grief, Helping Family Members Resolve Death, Dying, and Bereavement Issues,* NY: The Guilford Press, 2001.

Caplan, Sandi and Gordon Lang, *Grief's Courageous Journey, A Workbook,* Oakland, CA.: New Harbinger Publications, Inc., 1995.

James, John W. and Russell Friedman, *The Grief Recovery Handbook, The Action Program for Moving Beyond Death, Divorce, and Other Losses,* NY: HarperPerennial, 1998.

Kubler-Ross, Elisabeth, David Kessler, *On Grief and Grieving, Finding the Meaning of Grief Through the Five Stages of Loss,* Waterville, Maine: Thorndike Press, 2005.

Kumar, Sameet, *Grieving Mindfully, A Compassionate and Spiritual Guide to Coping with Loss,* Oakland, CA.: New Harbinger Publications, Inc., 2005.

Moody, Raymond Jr., Dianne Arcangel, *Life After Loss, Conquering Grief and Finding Hope,* San Francisco, CA.: HarperSanFrancisco, 2001.

Tousley, Marty, www.griefhealing.com.

NOT GOOD ENOUGH

Not Good Enough

Feeling not good enough or "less than" is played out in a cycle of shame, hopelessness, and self-pity. We feel shame about who we are, that we have little value, and that we are not good enough. Feeling "less than" spirals down into depression, self-sabotage, and survival.

Not being good enough creates an illusion of fear...fear of being rejected, abandoned, left out, and/or forgotten.

Feeling not good enough, feeling less than, feeling sorry for ourselves, and feeling hopeless keeps us stuck in survival. When in survival, it is risky to step outside our comfort zone. Thus the pattern repeats itself over and over and over.

When we feel less than and not good enough, our self-worth and self-esteem is lacking. Self esteem is the ability to earn love. When self-esteem is lacking, we lack self respect, pride, and self love.

When we don't feel good enough, we lack self love and self esteem. We don't love ourselves and we cannot earn love. The result? Anger, frustration, grief, self pity, hurt, shame, apathy, helplessness, and hopelessness...

Mis-belief Tapping Statements for Not Good Enough

1. I hate myself.
2. I don't matter.
3. I don't belong.
4. I am a mistake.
5. I am not lovable.
6. I'm not authentic.
7. Life is a struggle.
8. I feel dead inside.
9. I lack self-esteem.
10. I lack self-respect.
11. I don't like myself.
12. I am less than others.
13. I wish I were invisible.
14. I feel less than others.
15. I don't nurture myself.
16. I am inferior to others.
17. I deflect compliments.
18. I don't know who I am.
19. I am not good enough.
20. I will never be enough.
21. I need other's approval.
22. I am not lovable as I am.
23. I have no value or worth.
24. Other people ignore me.
25. I am undeserving of love.

> A lot of people say they want to get out of pain, and I'm sure that's true, but they aren't willing to make healing a high priority. They aren't willing to look inside to see the source of their pain in order to deal with it.
>
> Lindsay Wagner

1. From the previous page, list the seven statements that you thought or felt applied to you:

1.

2.

3.

4.

5.

6.

7.

2. Select one of the statements from above and describe how it plays out in your life. Give an example or two. It is important to recognize and identify the pattern. Is there a trigger? How does it begin? How has it benefited you? How has it harmed you? For instance, are you lovable as you are? Or do you have to prove you are lovable by doing something noteworthy?

3. Tap the seven statements above. If more than seven applied, tap them as well.

4. As you were tapping, did you have any new thoughts, memories of the past surface, any additional insights, and/or an ah-ah awareness?

26. What I do is not good enough.
27. I will be rejected for who I am.
28. I overeat to fill the void inside.
29. I overeat when I feel less than.
30. It is critical that others like me.
31. I must do everything perfectly.
32. I have no inner sense of worth.
33. I doubt my abilities and talents.
34. I live in a constant state of fear.
35. I feel selfish fulfilling my needs.
36. I am not accepted for who I am.
37. I doubt my abilities and talents.
38. I am seldom loved for who I am.
39. I allow others to manipulate me.
40. I must avoid mistakes at all cost.
41. I am overly sensitive to criticism.
42. I can love others but not myself.
43. I will never be as good as others.
44. I am overly sensitive to rejection.
45. My approval of me is not enough.
46. I'm filled with fear and self-doubt.
47. My wounds are too deep to heal.
48. I'm defective, broken, and flawed.
49. Being imperfect is not acceptable.
50. I eat when I feel inferior to others.

> When we hold someone responsible for what we experience, we lose power. When we depend upon another person for the experiences we think are necessary to our well-being, we live continually in the fear that they will not deliver.
>
> Gary Zukav

1. From the previous page, list the seven statements that you thought or felt applied to you:

1.

2.

3.

4.

5.

6.

7.

2. Select one of the statements from above and describe how it plays out in your life. Give an example or two. It is important to recognize and identify the pattern. Is there a trigger? How does it begin? How has it benefited you? How has it harmed you? For instance, are you filled with fear and self-doubt? Is this your excuse for not learning new skills? Is it easier to be a coward than to apply yourself learning new skills?

3. Tap the seven statements above. If more than seven applied, tap them as well.

4. As you were tapping, did you have any new thoughts, memories of the past surface, any additional insights, and/or an ah-ah awareness?

51. I wish I could be invisible.
52. I'm not gifted at anything.
53. I'm afraid of being judged.
54. I am not deserving of love.
55. I am the scum of the earth.
56. I am ordinary in every way.
57. I am last on my priority list.
58. I am broken beyond repair.
59. I have no value as a person.
60. Who I am is not acceptable.
61. I depend on others for love.
62. I beat myself up when I fail.
63. I am not gentle with myself.
64. I am not in charge of my life.
65. I will never be good enough.
66. I am inferior to other people.
67. I don't love or accept myself.
68. I feel shame most of the time.
69. I avoid challenging situations.
70. I am not deserving of respect.
71. I blame myself for everything.
72. I overeat when I feel unloved.
73. I don't make myself a priority.
74. I have no control over my life.
75. I overeat when I feel ordinary.

> Less than and not good enough destroy hope and keep us lost in maze called "survival." The only way out of survival is to heal the feeling of not being good enough. The only way to change not being good enough is to heal the underlying beliefs.
>
> Tessa Cason

1. From the previous page, list the seven statements that you thought or felt applied to you:

1.

2.

3.

4.

5.

6.

7.

2. Select one of the statements from above and describe how it plays out in your life. Give an example or two. It is important to recognize and identify the pattern. Is there a trigger? How does it begin? How has it benefited you? How has it harmed you? For instance, are you not in charge of my life? If not, do you play the blame game? "It's their fault I can't have what I want!" When you blame and are not in charge of your life, you don't take ownership of your life. Is it easier to be the victim or victor?

3. Tap the seven statements above. If more than seven applied, tap them as well.

4. As you were tapping, did you have any new thoughts, memories of the past surface, any additional insights, and/or an ah-ah awareness?

76. I am powerless to create the life I want.
77. I cover up my feelings of unworthiness.
78. I feel humiliated when I make a mistake.
79. I feel alone, invisible, and disconnected.
80. Others see as me as flawed and inferior.
81. I am constantly finding fault with myself.
82. I cannot accept compliments graciously.
83. I feel inadequate, unworthy, and inferior.
84. The real me stays hidden from everyone.
85. I don't feel deserving, worthy, or lovable.
86. I use my weight to avoid moving forward.
87. I am a victim to whom things just happen.
88. I am angry at myself for being overweight.
89. My self-talk is more negative than positive.
90. I don't accept full responsibility for my life.
91. I am not comfortable around other people.
92. I don't have conscious control of my habits.
93. I don't deserve the good I desire and want.
94. I am susceptible to the negativity of others.
95. I am obligated to fulfill the needs of others.
96. I go overboard doing nice things for others.
97. I am constantly comparing myself to others.
98. I think more highly of others than of myself.
99. Nothing I do will ever make me feel worthy.
100. I overeat when I feel I am not good enough.

Experience is a hard teacher. She gives the test first, the lesson afterwards.

Vernon Sanders Law

1. From the previous page, list the seven statements that you thought or felt applied to you:

1.

2.

3.

4.

5.

6.

7.

2. Select one of the statements from above and describe how it plays out in your life. Give an example or two. It is important to recognize and identify the pattern. Is there a trigger? How does it begin? How has it benefited you? How has it harmed you? For instance, do you use your weight to avoid moving forward? If it wasn't weight, would it be something else? Is it easier to stagnate than have goals and commit to the goals? Does the thought of moving forward feel like stepping into a dark forest without a flashlight?

3. Tap the seven statements above. If more than seven applied, tap them as well.

4. As you were tapping, did you have any new thoughts, memories of the past surface, any additional insights, and/or an ah-ah awareness?

101. I am easily hurt and oversensitive.
102. I feel shame that I am overweight.
103. I am embarrassed by compliments.
104. I am not a valuable, unique person.
105. I am not comfortable being myself.
106. I criticize, dislike, and reject myself.
107. I have little value as a human being.
108. I am not important and don't matter.
109. I am full of self-doubt and insecurity.
110. I am not special enough to be loved.
111. I turn errors into major catastrophes.
112. I don't love, honor, or cherish myself.
113. I expect the worst to always happen.
114. I have nothing of value to contribute.
115. I am critical of myself and my actions.
116. My fatness confirms my lack of worth.
117. I feel defeated, beaten, and bankrupt.
118. I should do what others expect of me.
119. It upsets me when others criticize me.
120. Others are more intelligent than I am.
121. It is selfish for me to want what I want.
122. There are many things wrong with me.
123. I have nothing special to offer anyone.
124. I am excessively demanding of myself.
125. My happiness does not depend on me.

> Men and women are limited not by the place of their birth, not by the color of their skin, but by the size of their hope.
>
> John Johnson

1. From the previous page, list the seven statements that you thought or felt applied to you:

1.

2.

3.

4.

5.

6.

7.

2. Select one of the statements from above and describe how it plays out in your life. Give an example or two. It is important to recognize and identify the pattern. Is there a trigger? How does it begin? How has it benefited you? How has it harmed you? For instance, do you expect the worst to always happen and then it does? Are you present in your life? Mishaps happen when we are not in present time. If we are not in present time, we are either in the future with our fears, or the past with our anger. Where are you?

3. Tap the seven statements above. If more than seven applied, tap them as well.

4. As you were tapping, did you have any new thoughts, memories of the past surface, any additional insights, and/or an ah-ah awareness?

126. I fall short every time I compare myself to others.
127. I must make my loved one's need my first priority.
128. I don't listen to my own wishes, goals, and dreams.
129. I feel powerless, weak, and vulnerable all the time.
130. Not being accepted leads to my being overweight.
131. I am not as good, worthy, or as deserving as others.
132. I don't accept myself unconditionally exactly as I am.
133. I often feel out of place, uncomfortable, and anxious.
134. Not feeling worthwhile leads to my being overweight.
135. I become very uncomfortable when others criticize me.
136. I make other people's needs more important than mine.
137. I feel insecure and uncomfortable around other people.
138. It is important that most people like and approve of me.
139. I cannot approve of myself unless others approve of me.
140. There is something wrong with me that others dislike me.
141. Overeating is synonymous with shame and worthlessness.
142. Others are superior to me because of their achievements.
143. Difficulty in my relationships lead to my being overweight.
144. I cannot ask others directly what I want or need from them.
145. My worth as a person is related to how well I do everything.
146. It is inconsiderate not to do what others ask me to do for them.
147. Other's opinions of me are more important than my opinion of me.
148. I allow others to verbally, emotionally, and/or physically abuse me.
149. I let others make me feel guilty when I don't do what they ask of me.
150. I am not free to say no when others make unreasonable demands of me.

> Our greatest weakness lies in giving up. The most certain way to succeed is always to try just one more time.
>
> Thomas Edison

1. From the previous page, list the seven statements that you thought or felt applied to you:

1.

2.

3.

4.

5.

6.

7.

2. Select one of the statements from above and describe how it plays out in your life. Give an example or two. It is important to recognize and identify the pattern. Is there a trigger? How does it begin? How has it benefited you? How has it harmed you? For instance, is it inconsiderate not to do what others ask you to do for them? Is this about the fear of being rejected? Does your worth come from being the "go-to-guy?" Or maybe it is about needing to please everyone.

3. Tap the seven statements above. If more than seven applied, tap them as well.

4. As you were tapping, did you have any new thoughts, memories of the past surface, any additional insights, and/or an ah-ah awareness?

151. Those with titles are more worthy than I am.
152. There is something basically wrong with me.
153. Others see me as defective, flawed, and bad.
154. I am not in charge of my life or my behaviors.
155. My worth is related to how well I do anything.
156. Being rejected leads to my being overweight.
157. I am super-sensitive to criticism and rejection.
158. I need to boast and prove my worth to others.
159. I can't defend myself when others criticize me.
160. I berate myself for my real and imagined flaws.
161. Being overweight proves I am less than others.
162. My worth comes from what I can do for others.
163. Not being loved leads to my being overweight.
164. I give into my food cravings when I feel flawed.
165. Those with degrees are more worthy than I am.
166. I'm worthless unless I do well and please others.
167. I overeat when my needs are not being fulfilled.
168. Other's needs are more important than my own.
169. I am afraid of being rejected and/or abandoned.
170. I hate that others judge me based on my weight.
171. Feeling worthless leads to my being overweight.
172. Not being wanted leads to my being overweight.
173. My needs are less important than my loved ones.
174. I would be rejected if I let others see the real me.
175. I am "less than" when I compare myself to others.

> Don't measure yourself by what you've accomplished, but rather by what you should have accomplished with your abilities.
>
> John Wooden

1. From the previous page, list the seven statements that you thought or felt applied to you:

1.

2.

3.

4.

5.

6.

7.

2. Select one of the statements from above and describe how it plays out in your life. Give an example or two. It is important to recognize and identify the pattern. Is there a trigger? How does it begin? How has it benefited you? How has it harmed you? For instance, do you wear yourself out pleasing other people? Are you available 24/7? Would it be selfish to put yourself first? Or are you not important enough to put yourself first?

3. Tap the seven statements above. If more than seven applied, tap them as well.

4. As you were tapping, did you have any new thoughts, memories of the past surface, any additional insights, and/or an ah-ah awareness?

Bibliography

Carter-Scott, Cherie, *If Love is a Game, These are the Rules,* New York: Broadway Books, 1999.

Minchinton, Jerry, *Maximum Self-Esteem,* Vanznat, MO: Arnford House Publishers, 1993.

Wegscheider-Cruse, Sharon, *Learning to Love Yourself,* Deerfield Beach, FL: Health Communications, Inc., 1987.

FAILURE

Failure

The opposite of failure is success. By examining what successful people do, we might be able to determine where our failure occurs or at least, what is contributing to our failure.

Even though success is different for each of us, there are common threads throughout all successes. Here are some of the common threads:

Successful people:

* Know what they want.

* Allow themselves to dream.

* Set goals and work toward their fulfillment.

* Have a detailed plan to accomplish their goals and dreams.

* Take action.

* Understand that setbacks and obstacles will teach them valuable lessons.

* Focus on solutions and are solution-oriented.

* Know everything they accomplish in life is up to them.

* Take complete responsibility for their lives.

* Don't quit or give up.

* Understand there is no guarantee they will succeed.

* Are flexible about the process of achieving their goals.

* Make decisions and continue to move forward.

* Continually reevaluate their plan.

* Accept change and adapt to difficulties.

* Are resilient and persistent.

* Believe in their success before success is visible.

* Are willing to accept feedback and self-correct.

* Are committed to the fulfillment of their dreams and goals.

* Live in the "now." They are present in their lives.

* Know that life is not a rehearsal for something else.

* Understand the seeds they plant today will be the rewards they will harvest tomorrow.

* Expect to meet many obstacles and difficulties along the way.

* Know that failure is only temporary, just part of the process.

* Pick themselves up after failure and press on.

Successful people are dreamers with their feet firmly planted in reality. The challenge of working toward their dreams and goals is just as exciting as the fulfillment of them. Overcoming each obstacle strengthens their resolve. Each lesson they learn from failure brings them closer to success. Their focus is on the goal. Successful people know they will succeed before there is evidence of their success.

* Failure is about LACK. Lack of power, persistence, courage, confidence, skills, knowledge, talent, etc., etc., etc.
* Failure is about the willingness to stay stuck in hopelessness and helplessness.
* Failure is giving up and feeling this is the best it will ever be.

WE FAIL WHEN WE DON'T CREATE THE REALITY WE DESIRE.

The 7 Pay-offs for not creating our reality are:

Avoidance

Blame

Self pity

Guarantee

Self Importance

Self Righteous

Cling to the Past

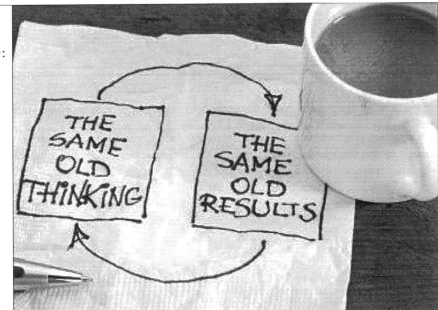

MIS-BELIEF TAPPING STATEMENTS FOR FAILURE

1. I fail every diet.

2. All diets fail me.

3. I set myself up to fail.

4. I search for quick fixes.

5. I am an emotional eater.

6. I am a forever pessimist.

7. I blow every diet I go on.

8. I am a weight loss failure.

9. Fatness runs in my family.

10. I gave up a long time ago.

11. My goals are not realistic.

12. My goals are unattainable.

13. I'm not able to lose weight.

14. Setbacks mean I have failed.

15. I stay down when I fall down.

16. I will start my diet tomorrow.

17. I am not excite about my life.

18. I often feel inferior to others.

19. I will fail at weight loss if I try.

20. I don't have a plan for my life.

21. I am intimidated by obstacles.

22. My identity is that of a failure.

23. I don't face my fears head on.

24. I avoid living life to the fullest.

25. I blame others for my failures.

> Always bear in mind that your own resolution to succeed is more important than any other one thing.
>
> Abraham Lincoln

1. From the previous page, list the seven statements that you thought or felt applied to you:

1.

2.

3.

4.

5.

6.

7.

2. Select one of the statements from above and describe how it plays out in your life. Give an example or two. It is important to recognize and identify the pattern. Is there a trigger? How does it begin? How has it benefited you? How has it harmed you? For instance, are your goals realistic? If not, then do you even try? Is this your excuse for not trying? Do you feel empowered to create your goals? Are you willing to work toward your goals? Or are you too insecure to pursue that which you really desire?

3. Tap the seven statements above. If more than seven applied, tap them as well.

4. As you were tapping, did you have any new thoughts, memories of the past surface, any additional insights, and/or an ah-ah awareness?

26. I don't celebrate my little successes.
27. It is not okay/safe to make mistakes.
28. I lack the self-control to lose weight.
29. I lack the tools and skills to be loved.
30. I lack the self-esteem to lose weight.
31. I will never succeed at losing weight.
32. Others will reject me if I lose weight.
33. I lack the courage to live my life fully.
34. I have given up on myself and my life.
35. I lack the commitment to lose weight.
36. I lack the focus needed to lose weight.
37. I don't eat foods that nourish my body.
38. I protect myself from disappointments.
39. I can't handle another disappointment.
40. I don't exercise enough to lose weight.
41. I give up when obstacles block my way.
42. I've given up on my dreams and myself.
43. Losing weight will always be a struggle.
44. I continue to indulge after I messed up.
45. I don't know how to deal with setbacks.
46. I am destined to be overweight forever.
47. I can't resist the foods I crave the most.
48. I am not committed to being successful.
49. Setbacks are not opportunities to grow.
50. I can't lose weight because of my genes.

> Anger is about the past. Fear is about the future. Fear may actually be anger that we will fail again in the future.
>
> Tessa Cason

1. From the previous page, list the seven statements that you thought or felt applied to you:

1.

2.

3.

4.

5.

6.

7.

2. Select one of the statements from above and describe how it plays out in your life. Give an example or two. It is important to recognize and identify the pattern. Is there a trigger? How does it begin? How has it benefited you? How has it harmed you? For instance, do you feel there is nothing good about mistakes? Do you have to be perfect and do everything perfectly? Does your perfectionism have you so locked in place that you are not able to change, progress, or learn from your mistakes?

3. Tap the seven statements above. If more than seven applied, tap them as well.

4. As you were tapping, did you have any new thoughts, memories of the past surface, any additional insights, and/or an ah-ah awareness?

51. I make excuses for my failures.
52. I am intimidated by challenges.
53. I don't have a vision for my life.
54. I focus on how far I have to go.
55. I am helpless to change my life.
56. I blame my problems on others.
57. I don't know exactly what I want.
58. I don't rebound from my failures.
59. My identity is struggle and diets.
60. I have no control over what I eat.
61. I have no willpower around food.
62. I lack the tenacity to lose weight.
63. I lack the courage to lose weight.
64. Those around me want me to fail.
65. I don't recover from my setbacks.
66. My identity is that of a fat person.
67. I lack the patience to lose weight.
68. I don't have a strategy for my life.
69. I procrastinate and make excuses.
70. I lack the discipline to lose weight.
71. I am apathetic about losing weight.
72. I lack the motivation to lose weight.
73. My overeating proves I am a failure.
74. It is impossible for me to eat health.
75. I give up too easily on losing weight.

> People are like guided missiles. Without a target, they wander aimlessly across the horizons and eventually self-destruct.
>
> Edge Keynote

1. From the previous page, list the seven statements that you thought or felt applied to you:

1.

2.

3.

4.

5.

6.

7.

2. Select one of the statements from above and describe how it plays out in your life. Give an example or two. It is important to recognize and identify the pattern. Is there a trigger? How does it begin? How has it benefited you? How has it harmed you? For instance, is it impossible to eat health? Is it the taste of healthy food you don't like? Is it the time to prepare healthy foods? What is it about eating healthy that is difficult? Or is that the excuse so you can continue to indulge in fast food and foods you crave?

3. Tap the seven statements above. If more than seven applied, tap them as well.

4. As you were tapping, did you have any new thoughts, memories of the past surface, any additional insights, and/or an ah-ah awareness?

76. I don't know how to deal with my frustrations.
77. I am too much of a pessimist to be successful.
78. I will never be able to sustain my ideal weight.
79. I'm a victim when it comes to food and eating.
80. I lack the self confidence weight loss requires.
81. My goals are not within my realm of capability.
82. I haven't taken responsibility for my health yet.
83. The only way to lose weight is to starve myself.
84. I'm not willing to do what I must to lose weight.
85. I don't know how to deal with disappointments.
86. Joy comes after successfully losing the weight.
87. It's difficult for me to stay positive after defeat.
88. I lack the positive attitude weight loss requires.
89. I lack the determination to keep on keeping on.
90. Disappointments are not opportunities to learn.
91. I'm not consistent in pursuing a health program.
92. After losing weight, I regain all the weight I lost.
93. I cannot overcome my defects and deficiencies.
94. I lack the motivation to successfully lose weight.
95. I am not committed to losing the excess weight.
96. I am not willing to put forth extraordinary effort.
97. I would have to examine my life to be successful.
98. I won't be able to relate to others if I lost weight.
99. I lack the persistence to successfully lose weight.
100. I can't lose weight because of my body chemistry.

> Failure is the opportunity to begin again more intelligently.
>
> Henry Ford

1. From the previous page, list the seven statements that you thought or felt applied to you:

1.

2.

3.

4.

5.

6.

7.

2. Select one of the statements from above and describe how it plays out in your life. Give an example or two. It is important to recognize and identify the pattern. Is there a trigger? How does it begin? How has it benefited you? How has it harmed you? For instance, are you disgusted with your body? The body we have is the vessel we have been given to move through life. Your car is the vehicle you move around on the roadways. What condition is your car? Do you trash your car as much as you trash your body? Is it easier to trash your body than to do the work to have the body you want?

3. Tap the seven statements above. If more than seven applied, tap them as well.

4. As you were tapping, did you have any new thoughts, memories of the past surface, any additional insights, and/or an ah-ah awareness?

101. I can't figure out what I am doing wrong.
102. I don't know how to overcome obstacles.
103. I'm powerless to stop gorging when I eat.
104. I lack the tools and skills to be successful.
105. It is impossible for me to lose this weight.
106. I don't have the energy to change my life.
107. It's too hard to stop the emotional eating.
108. I don't learn valuable lessons from defeat.
109. I don't know how to overcome difficulties.
110. I lack the desire to lose the excess weight.
111. I don't know how to learn from my failures.
112. I don't have the courage to change my life.
113. I lack the mental toughness to lose weight.
114. My food choices are made by my emotions.
115. I don't know how to get to there from here.
116. I'm not capable of losing the excess weight.
117. It is hopeless that anything will work for me.
118. It is impossible for me to succeed at dieting.
119. I'm not committed to a total health program.
120. I use every excuse so I can indulge in eating.
121. I don't know how to overcome loss or defeat.
122. I will never be able to lose the excess weight.
123. I can't lose weight because of my upbringing.
124. Failure cannot teach me valuable life lessons.
125. I can't lose weight because of my personality.

> There are no secrets to success. It is the result of preparation, hard work, and learning from failure.
>
> Colin Powell

1. From the previous page, list the seven statements that you thought or felt applied to you:

1.

2.

3.

4.

5.

6.

7.

2. Select one of the statements from above and describe how it plays out in your life. Give an example or two. It is important to recognize and identify the pattern. Is there a trigger? How does it begin? How has it benefited you? How has it harmed you? For instance, does your lack of success confirm your inadequacy? Is this about self-worth, success, learning new skills, and/or working toward a goal? Or that you lack the tools and skills to be successful?

3. Tap the seven statements above. If more than seven applied, tap them as well.

126. My weight is an impossible obstacle to overcome.
127. I lack the inner strength necessary to lose weight.
128. I don't have a clear vision of my weight loss goals.
129. I don't know how to re-chart my path after defeat.
130. Losing weight pushes me out of my comfort zone.
131. I don't have the courage to weigh my ideal weight.
132. I have failed every time I have tried to lose weight.
133. It is impossible for me to succeed at losing weight.
134. My health and well-being are not my top priorities.
135. I have tried and failed so many time to lose weight.
136. I have given up hope that my life will ever improve.
137. It is hopeless that I will ever weigh my ideal weight.
138. I'm not totally committed to a weight loss program.
139. I will regain back all the weight I lose after losing it.
140. I don't have what it takes to succeed at weight loss.
141. I lack the determination to successfully lose weight.
142. I am not committed to permanent lifestyle changes.
143. I'm not motivated enough to lose the excess weight.
144. I don't have the determination to overcome setbacks.
145. Thinking about losing weight puts me into overwhelm.
146. I have failed at every attempt to heal my weight issues.
147. No matter what I do, I will never be able to lose weight.
148. I don't have the mental toughness weight loss requires.
149. Feeling stupid and dumb leads to my being overweight.
150. I'm doing everything right and still can't lose the weight.

> You are unique and if that is not fulfilled, then something wonderful has been lost.
>
> Martha Graham

1. From the previous page, list the seven statements that you thought or felt applied to you:

1.

2.

3.

4.

5.

6.

7.

2. Select one of the statements from above and describe how it plays out in your life. Give an example or two. It is important to recognize and identify the pattern. Is there a trigger? How does it begin? How has it benefited you? How has it harmed you? For instance, will you regain back the weight you lose after losing it? 95% of people that do lose weight put the weight back on. The odds are in favor of gaining it back...UNLESS, you change the dysfunctional, mis-beliefs on a subconscious level. Healing the beliefs change the thoughts, feelings, actions, reactions, choices, and decisions we make about food.

3. Tap the seven statements above. If more than seven applied, tap them as well.

4. As you were tapping, did you have any new thoughts, memories of the past surface, any additional insights, and/or an ah-ah awareness?

151. I don't have short-term realistic goals to lose the weight.
152. I don't have the perseverance that losing weight requires.
153. I will never be able to permanently weigh my ideal weight.
154. I would have to take ownership of my life to be successful.
155. Too much conflicting information to be able to lose weight.
156. I lack the patience necessary to improve my life and health.
157. Thinking about all my failures leads to my being overweight.
158. I lack the discipline necessary to improve my life and health.
159. I lack the inner strength needed to successfully lose weight.
160. I cannot see myself completing and accomplishing my goals.
161. I am under too much stress to successful work on my health.
162. I lack the motivation to continue when the going gets rough.
163. I don't have the patience to stick to my weight loss program.
164. Not being in control of my life leads to my being overweight.
165. It takes too much energy and effort to reach my ideal weight.
166. I don't know which plan is the best plan for me to lose weight.
167. Something always sabotages my commitment to losing weight.
168. I don't have the persistence to stick to my weight loss program.
169. I don't have the courage to make permanent changes in my life.
170. I don't have the energy to explore buried feelings about my life.
171. Problems are overwhelming obstacles I am unable to overcome.
172. I don't have the self-control to maintain my weight loss program.
173. I deprive my body of the nourishing foods it needs to sustain life.
174. I don't have the self-discipline to maintain my weight loss program.
175. I lack the serious commitment needed to improve my life and health.

The road to success has many tempting parking places.

Steve Potter

1. From the previous page, list the seven statements that you thought or felt applied to you:

1.

2.

3.

4.

5.

6.

7.

2. Select one of the statements from above and describe how it plays out in your life. Give an example or two. It is important to recognize and identify the pattern. Is there a trigger? How does it begin? How has it benefited you? How has it harmed you? For instance, does something always sabotages your commitment to losing weight? Have you noticed the one common denominator? That would be you!

3. Tap the seven statements above. If more than seven applied, tap them as well.

4. As you were tapping, did you have any new thoughts, memories of the past surface, any additional insights, and/or an ah-ah awareness?

BIBLIOGRAPHY

Canfield, Jack and Janet Switzer, *The Success Principles: How to Get from Where You Are to Where You Want to Be*, NY: William Morrow, 2004.

Canfield, Jack and Mark Victor Hansen, Les Hewitt, *The Power of Focus: What the Worlds Greatest Achievers Know about The Secret of Financial Freedom and Success,* Deerfield Beach, FL: Health Communications, Inc., 2000.

Carter-Scott, Cherie, *If Success is a Game, These are the Rules,* New York: Broadway Books, 2000.

Gladwell, Malcolm, *Outliers: The Story of Success,* NY: Little, Brown and Company, 2008.

Newberry, Tommy, *Success Is Not an Accident: Change Your Choices; Change Your Life,* Carol Stream, IL: Tyndale House Publishers; 2007.

Newberry, Tommy, *The 4:8 Principle: The Secret to a Joy-filled Life,* Carol Stream, IL: Tyndale House Publishers; 2007.

Taylor, Sandra Anne and Sharon A. Klingler, *Secrets of Success: The Science and Spirit of Real Prosperity,* Carlsbad, CA: Hay House, 2008.

About the Author – Tessa Cason, MA

I have been fortunate to have had a number of successful professional lives. In each of these endeavors, it provided the opportunity to observe someone's behavior, actions, reactions, habits, thoughts, feelings, choices, and decisions. Understanding who we are, how we became who we are, and how to change into who we want to become has been a fascinating area of study and research for me for 50 years.

As a swim coach and instructor of 10 and under kids, I had the opportunity to teach and train small children. As an instructor of PE at San Diego State University and Grossmont College, I had the opportunity to interact with and teach college-age individuals. As an owner of a gift company, I had the opportunity to work with business professionals. Belonging to a breakfast group called The Inside Edge and staffing events for The Learning Annex, I was able to interact with and observe the elite authors, speakers, and politicians. Managing a medical clinic provided the opportunity to interact with and observe the seriously ill, some terminal.

In 1977, as a hobby, I started a company that manufactured greeting cards and stationery. Eight years later, my company was grossing a million dollars in sale/year on 50 cent greeting cards.

When my business was grossing a million dollars in sale, I purchased a newly constructed townhouse in La Jolla. Unbeknownst to me, a natural gas pipe was severed during construction and not properly repaired. The gas leak went undetected for 2 1/2 years, 850 days. By then, my health was permanently damaged.

After the gas leak was discovered, all the doctors told me I would be environmentally ill for the rest of my life and would never be able to participate or function in the real world. Not believing the doctors, I set upon a course to discover alternative health treatments. Several years later, while still working on my health, I was managing an alternative health clinic. While working at the clinic, I was able to make the correlation between a patient's emotions and beliefs with their physical illnesses.

In 1996, after thirty years of book reading, psychology classes, metaphysical classes, lectures, and observation, I applied my knowledge and skills into a life coaching practice. I thoroughly enjoyed being a Transformational Life Coach, helping others find clarity in their lives.

Only one problem. It was this: The clients were not completing their assigned tasks that together we had decided they would do as their homework. Even though the clients knew what to do and wanted to do the tasks, somehow the tasks were not getting completed.

Knowing that all of our actions and reactions, thoughts and feelings, choices and decisions are based on our beliefs, I went searching for a tool that would change dysfunctional beliefs. I visited a friend that managed a bookstore and told her my dilemma and that I was in need of a tool, process, or technique that would change dysfunctional beliefs. She reached for a book that was on the counter, informing me that this new addition for them was flying off the shelves and their customers were raving about. It was a book on EFT (Emotional Freedom Technique) Tapping.

I read the book and ordered the videos. Even though I was intrigued, I had no clue how tapping my head could change dysfunctional beliefs or our lives. I had some adventuresome clients (and forgiving if need be) that I taught how to tap.

When every single client returned for their next appointment and shared how different their lives had been that week because of tapping, I took notice! My curiosity was peaked. I then put a lot of time and energy into figuring out how this powerful transformational tool, EFT Tapping, worked and how to best utilize EFT Tapping.

I soon realized working with my clients that the most important aspect of EFT Tapping was the statement that is said as we tap. I also realized that some of the statements I wrote up for one client could be used for another. My clients wanted homework, wanted tapping statements to do on their own. I started a library of EFT Tapping statements that I wrote out for my client as their homework.

In 2005 I was diagnosed with thyroid cancer. While researching thyroid cancer, I discovered that 20 years after exposure to natural gas, thyroid issues would result. It was 20 years nearly to the month that I started having thyroid issues.

From the time I was diagnosed and had surgery, those 6 weeks I only focused on the emotional issues associated with the thyroid and tapped. I did not pursue any other treatments, supplements, or therapies in the 6 weeks leading up to the surgery other than EFT Tapping.

In the recovery room after surgery, the surprised doctor told me that even though two different labs came back with the diagnoses of cancer, it was not cancer. I knew the tapping had changed the energy of the cancer and it no longer was cancer.

Our lives don't change until we change our programming...the beliefs on a subconscious level. EFT Tapping is one of the most powerful techniques I found that could do just that: change our beliefs on a subconscious level.

After surgery, knowing the power of EFT Tapping, knowing the significance of the tapping statement, and knowing that beliefs precede all of our thoughts and feelings, choices and decisions, actions, reactions, and experiences, I created 43 Books for Practitioners and 43 Workbooks for Everyone that were filled with mis-belief, dysfunctional EFT tapping statements.

Now, 2015, I am revamping the Workbooks. In the revamped Workbooks, I am combining tapping statements for 5 different topics in each theme-book to heal the issue as completely as possible.

I also have a series of "80 EFT Tapping Statement" Kindle eBooks on Amazon.

My two greatest joys are helping those that want to grow, evolve, and transform their lives and train others to be transformational coaches!

Books and Kindles eBooks by Tessa Cason

80 EFT Tapping Statements for:
Abandonment
Abundance, Wealth, Money
Addictions
Adult Children of Alcoholics
Anger and Frustration
Anxiety and Worry
Change
"Less Than" and Anxiety
Manifesting a Romantic Relationship
Relationship with Self
Self Esteem
Social Anxiety
Weight and Emotional Eating

EFT Tapping Statements for:
A Broken Heart, Abandonment, Anger, Depression, Grief, Emotional Healing
Anxiety, Fear, Anger, Self Pity, Change
Champion, Success, Personal Power, Self Confidence, Leader/Role Model
PTSD, Disempowered, Survival, Fear, Anger
Weight & Food Cravings, Anger, Grief, Not Good Enough, Failure

Other Books
Why we Crave What We Crave: The Archetypes of Food Cravings
How to Heal Our Food Cravings

EFT WORKBOOK AND JOURNAL FOR EVERYONE:

Abandonment

Abundance, Money, Prosperity

Addictions

Adult Children of Alcoholics

Anger, Apathy, Guilt

Anxiety/Worry

Being A Man

Being, Doing, Belonging

Champion

Change

Conflict

Courage

Dark Forces

Decision Making

Depression

Difficult/Toxic Parents

Difficult/Toxic People

Emotional Healing

Fear

Forgiveness

God

Grief

Happiness/Joy

Intuition

Leadership

Live Your Dreams

Life Purpose/Mission

People Pleaser

Perfectionism

Personal Power

Relationship w/Others

Relationship w/Self & Commitment to Self

Self Confidence

Self Worth/Esteem

Sex

Shame

Stress

Success

Survival

Transitions

Trust/Discernment

Victim, Self-pity, Self-Defeating Behavior, Shadow Self

Weight and Emotional Eating

MIS-BELIEF EFT STATEMENTS FOR PRACTITIONERS:

Abandonment
Abundance, Money, Prosperity
Addictions
Adult Children of Alcoholics
Anger, Apathy, Guilt
Anxiety/Worry
Being A Man
Being, Doing, Belonging
Champion
Change
Conflict
Courage
Dark Forces
Decision Making
Depression
Difficult/Toxic Parents
Difficult/Toxic People
Emotional Healing
Fear
Forgiveness
God
Grief
Happiness/Joy
Intuition
Leadership
Live Your Dreams
Life Purpose/Mission
People Pleaser
Perfectionism
Personal Power
Relationship w/Others
Relationship w/Self & Commitment w/Self
Self Confidence
Self Worth/Esteem
Sex
Shame
Stress
Success
Survival
Transitions
Trust/Discernment
Victim, Self-pity, Self-Defeating Behavior, Shadow Self
Weight and Emotional Eating

Testimonial for Tessa EFT Tapping Books and Workbooks

"I am a beginning practitioner. I knew I needed additional resources to use with my clients. I found Tessa's ebooks online and purchased several ebooks. Having a step-by-step process has really helped my confidence level. My clients are having success as well."

"EFT is a remarkable tool. Working with Tessa's mis-belief statements has made my job easier."

HERE IS WHAT OTHERS HAVE SAID ABOUT USING TESSA'S BOOKS FOR EVERYONE:

"It was 2003 and I had just suffered a devastating divorce. I felt as if I was on my knees before the Universe when someone recommended Tessa to me. We began working with the mis-beliefs for Survival as I was almost unable to function. My personal growth grew in leaps and bounds and I now have a thriving business along with an amazing marriage."

"I had tried everything to help my increasing anxiety problems. I was almost incapacitated by situations that were common, everyday events to most people. I had tried several prescription drugs, traditional therapy, several self-help books, even alcohol, and nothing worked. Out of sheer desperation I decided to try EFT and one of Tessa's workbook. I thought EFT was a strange process at first, but a week after my first session I was able to make it through an entire workout at the gym without a panic attack or even one heart palpitation! It continues to amaze me how effective EFT and working with Tessa's books have been."

"I am writing to express my most gracious appreciation for your work. You are one of God's most profound Light Workers. In just 2 sessions, I have let go of a great deal of blocked energy and re-focused my life in directions I could not have imagined. Your work with EFT can, literally, save everyone years on their healing journey. Superb!"

With Gratitude and Appreciation

There are several people I would like to thank:

* I am thankful for Roger Callahan's, Gary Craig's, and Pat Carrington's work developing TFT and EFT. Without their willingness to break the mold, we might still be lying on the couch telling our stories rather than healing our hearts and mis-beliefs.

* I am very thankful for my clients in 2000 that were willing to try something new, something untested, something that was outside the norm. I learned so much watching their growth and evolution.

* I am thankful for Nick Ortner and The Tapping Solution. Nick is willing to defend EFT Tapping and brave the way for the rest of us.

* I am thankful for the research that Dawson Church has put into legitimizing EFT Tapping.

* I am thankful for all the practitioners and people that believe and continue to tap even though it is not quite widely accepted yet.

41041345R10101

Made in the USA
Middletown, DE
02 March 2017